THE MACKESON
BOOK OF
AVERAGES

ROBERT PORTER

ANDRE DEUTSCH

With Cartoons by

Albert

Banx

Dickinson

Donegan

Dredge

Chic

Cotham

Duncan

ffolkes

Noel Ford

Handelsman

Heath

Holt

JAK

Jeeves

Gray Jolliffe

David Langdon

Larry

Mac

Mike Maurice

David Myers

Alan Parker

Ross

W Scully

Spencer

J W Taylor

Tibb

Mike Williams

Bob Wilson

First published 1985 by
André Deutsch Limited
105 Great Russell Street London WC1

ISBN 0 233 97844 5

Phototypeset by Kalligraphics Ltd
Printed in Great Britain by
R. J. Acford Chichester Sussex

THANKS & ACKNOWLEDGEMENTS

With this book, John Hegarty joins that small select band – which includes Archimedes and Hugh Hefner – who think of amazing things to do in their baths.

For it was in the Hegarty salle de bain that the *Mackeson Book of Averages* was conceived – in a classic flash of naked inspiration.

He could barely wait to offer it up to the Mackeson management. They enthusiastically moved the idea forward. Not for a moment did they think it odd that brewers of stout should be asked to consider a publishing venture.

Indeed the speed with which they went ahead is something which may well end up in that Record Book – you know the one.

The actual production of the book involved people and organisations too numerous to mention – information sources are listed at the back of the book – and my thanks go to all of them for putting their exceptional talents to such average use.

Robert Porter

Research

Organisation and collection of the research data was done by F.P. International, particularly John Flynn of that company. Special thanks are also owed to The Marketing Shop and BBC Data and Lawrence Publicity who contributed invaluable original research.

TRAINING THE AVERAGE DOG

Like that, see?

Why do we have to be so average, Norman?
We're always the 0.8% who leave before the end.

Contents

Introduction

What is Average?

YOU
At Birth
Early Years
Your Good Health
Weight and Height
Diseases
Accidents
Death

FAMILY
Household Size
Marital Status
Relatives

HOME
Household Expenditure
Shopping
Household Duties
Gas, Electricity, Telephone etc.

WORK
Hours Worked
Earnings
Type of Work
Executive Stress
Unemployment

LEISURE
TV and Radio
Cinema and Theatre

Reading
Sports and Games
Gardening
DIY
Holidays

SEX
First Partners
Pre-marital
The Wedding
Marriage
Extra-marital
Divorce
Remarriage
Homosexuality

SOCIAL
Eating and Drinking
Hygiene and Cosmetic
General Habits
Clothing
Pets
Motoring

EDUCATION
First Steps
Secondary
Further

RELIGION

POLITICS

AVERAGE QUIZ

AVERAGE TEENAGER?

I'm going to a fancy dress do, Dad – could I borrow your gear?

Introduction

What do you really think of yourself? Someone well . . . special . . . a cut above the norm? Or have you always had a deep conviction of your mediocrity? Perhaps you've always considered yourself run-of-the-mill, a common or garden variety.

Whichever of these opinions you hold, you are somehow choosing an Average — one which you are better or worse than, or the same as.

This book tells you where you really stand. You can compare yourself to everybody else in the country.

You can see whether you are on the right rung of the executive pay ladder; compare the frequency, place and quality of your sexual performance against millions of others; and while you are at it, check out your car, your pet, your visits to the doctor, and your telephone bill.

This book is indispensable for everyone.

Take those of you who have always won things — scholarships, victor laudorums and the like, who are now stars, bigwigs, captains of industry. You are unlikely to be modest. The revelation, through these chapters, that in so many ways and traits you are merely average, may be a chastening and character-building experience.

And what of you, slumped somewhere, thinking you are mediocre? Take heart, this book may reveal that with very little effort, you could be AVERAGE. And what could be more uplifting than finding out you are only as inadequate as everybody else?

As for you steeped in Averageness — who perhaps even consider your normality your prime virtue — these pages may well have a treat in store for you. They may reveal that you are the most average person in the United Kingdom. Do you see how wonderful that would be?

Your very averageness may have made you unique. You must celebrate this fact immediately. To be absolutely average is a transitory thing. Next week, next month you may slip out of this condition without even knowing it — perhaps by changing your present car for a Lada, or having a Daiquiri as your tipple.

Of course it is possible that you don't want to be average. Then you need this book to prove to yourself — and more importantly to convince others — that indeed you are much more than mean.

Here at last is the chance to position yourself. Read *The Mackeson Book of Averages* from cover to cover to find how average you are. Dip into it for reassurance when you think your standards are slipping — or rising.

Keep it nearby.

WHAT IS AVERAGE?

The dictionary defines average as that which is most common, a typical example of the group under discussion; or the arithmetic mean of a series. We use the word in both senses. If we can put a figure to the average, we do. Otherwise we use the word in its more popular sense.

AVERAGE WRONG INFORMATION IN THIS BOOK

One of the good things about averages is that they don't change as quickly as records. People are jumping higher and throwing things further almost every year, and beating the record.

Averages have a leisurely pace about them because they depend on everybody. For instance, if most babies finally grow up to be taller than their parents, it would still take a goodly time to affect the average height because of us already here.

But the fact that everybody goes into making an average is a major problem in itself because it means that one should measure, weigh and ask *everybody* to get the average height, weight and opinion. We have drawn from as many government and commercial sources and reports as we can. No doubt research published tomorrow will draw new conclusions. We suggest you add these findings to ours and divide by two.

So now read on – with the wealth of information before you, you may find yourself rich beyond the dreams of average!

A word about your class before we start.

You know how important it is to get these things right. Some years ago research agencies discarded the old-fashioned class definitions of posh, ordinary and common in favour of inoffensive letters from A to E. We have too.

AB's represent people well-placed in society and probably in professional employment. C_1 and C_2's the upper and lower halves of the middle class. D's and E's are what would have been called working-class before working became so fashionable.

The population is split: 20 per cent AB
50 per cent C_1 C_2
30 per cent DE

The average person is middle class.

AVERAGE ENGLISHMAN?

YOU – As an average baby

AVERAGE PREGNANCY

It's all any reasonable child can expect if the Dad is present at the conception. – Joe Orton

The average pregnancy lasts 266 days from conception. It's obviously easier to mark the right day on the calendar if you are one of those 970,000 who has sex less than once a month.

AVERAGE STAY IN HOSPITAL

The average woman stays only 5 days in hospital when having a baby.

AVERAGE BABY WEIGHT

I Thay! He'th Big!

The average baby weighs 7lb 5oz (3319gm).

It seems even this early on in our lives we know our place in the social order of things.

High birthweight babies, 8lb 13oz (over 4000gm), are much more likely to be born to the upper (not short of a) crust, AB strata.

Low birthweight babies, under 5lb 8oz (2500gm), are much commoner in commoners – in the lower social orders, DE's.

Babies of the middle classes, C_1 and C_2's, are usually of an average weight.

Shakespeare knew what he was about when he had Cymbeline say, 'There be many Caesars' . . . 11 per cent of all births in the UK are – a figure which has doubled in the last eight years. In America 20 per cent of all births are by caesarian section.

England Expects . . .

AVERAGE EXPECTATION
Britain expects

The average baby is expected. There's not the incredulous 'You can't be' as seen in old war films, where the hero's been a year at the front. 70 per cent of all pregnancies are deliberately planned by both parents. Only 15 per cent come as a surprise.

For people of a Henry VIII disposition, the disconcerting news is that most couples would prefer a girl.

The average mother-to-be does not follow a special diet but most will give up smoking — and drinking too; 60 per cent do. But 72 per cent don't give up work, they work before and during their pregnancy, up to the last month.

AVERAGE PRINCESS
Your Royal Averageness

The Princess of Wales is Mrs Average when it comes to planning her family — at least so far. Women aged between 20–24 usually have their first baby within the first or second year of marriage. Enter Prince William. Prince Harry was right on cue too as number two. Most couples have their second child within two or three years of the first.

Motherhood is beginning later, on average, due to the higher earnings of women keeping them at work longer. It is putting back the family by five years on average.

Only one in four couples go on to have a third or fourth; pre-war, one in five had four or more children like the Queen did. Perhaps some parents stop after three because they've heard that one child in every four is Chinese.

AVERAGE BIRTH WITNESSED
Did you see?

The average birth now has the father present. 75 per cent witness the birth of their children. It made husbands more loving and understanding, said 82 per cent of new mums. (It is not recorded whether any of the remaining 18 per cent said it made their husbands faint.)

In the beginning was the WAAAAAAA

The average bawling baby makes as much noise as a pneumatic drill — over 100 decibels.

AVERAGE BABY FOOD

Pretty soon we'll be putting him on fibres.

Abreast of the times

Now more than 70 per cent of babies are breast fed. Ten years ago it was less than 50 per cent.

EARLY TALENT

Smarty Pants

If you hope to beget a genius your average age as a father should be 36, and as a mother 31.

ENOUGH IS ENOUGH

Happiness is . . . the number of children you have

Most parents are happy with the number of children they have.

Only one in four women and one in five men would like more. One in six couples would like less – but they have, on average, more than four children.

FIRST CHILD

Waiting for Boyo? Not likely

The average parents do not wait until they can afford a baby. Only one in seven couples postpone having children because of the cost (which *is* high, see page 28). They want to get their house organised first. One couple in twenty-five have no choice about baby's arrival.

Most parents claim financial problems directly related to having children – but in fairness, children claim the same problem related to having parents.

AVERAGE NAMES

Is this the end for Janet and John?

First Name:

To be average your name is most likely to be James, or if you are a girl, Charlotte or Sarah. James has been the most popular boy's name for 21 years.

You've still a good chance of being average if your name is Edward or Thomas – if you're a boy this is! Or Emily or Victoria if you're a girl. These are all popular names.

If you are a William you have an additional advantage. It is among the most popular names for humans *and* dogs – so if you're trying to be the most average male and don't make it, how about trying to be the average pet?

But as these names are taken from *The Times* and *Daily Telegraph* announcements they can't be considered representative of the nation. A random supermarket survey may reveal a preponderance of Jasons, Brians, Sharons and Tracys. Presumably their parents don't tell *The Times* about them.

Alias Smith & . . .

Surnames:

As you may have guessed, you have to be a Smith to stand any chance of being really average. There are some 700,000 Smiths in the UK telephone directories, an estimated 900,000 in total – really bad news if you don't know the first name when you use Directory Enquiries.

Surnames Brown, Jones and Johnson nudge along at about half a million each with no serious chance of overtaking. The outsider coming up fast is Patel.

But sympathise with the Chinese. There are 75 million Chans. Obviously a case of the Inscrutable One in the sky looking down and saying 'Chans would be a fine thing'.

Any relation to the Willesden Smiths?

AVERAGE WALKING AGE

Until now you've always been a crawler

The average time it takes to take that small step for man but a giant one for babykind is 13 months. It is not surprising that it takes a year to get it together – every faltering step uses 54 muscles.

If he has a fault, it's the occasional split infinitive.

FIRST WORDS

Say it again, Sam

The average age of the first spoken word – beyond that stage known as vocalising – is 10 months. Usually to an outsider it sounds as if the infant is trying to pronounce unsorted Scrabble squares – but not to a proud parent.

And the reason it's important to understand this language, Babish, is the evidence that early speakers have higher IQs than average.

He said his first words yesterday – Phing! – Whump! – Whee! – Chakatta chakatta! and Blam!

Listen darling – his first word!

HEIGHT

The shape of things to come

The average child is half its adult height at the age of 2 years.

YOU: As an average child

CHILD MALADIES

The average child is 4.5 times more likely to catch measles, whooping cough or scarlet fever than the average adult. And three times more likely to get dysentery.

Poliomyelitis still carries a dread ring to its very name and most children, 84 per cent, are vaccinated against it. But these other diseases are contagious and dangerous and doctors would be pleased if we adopted the slogan 'get 'em vaccinated before the vacation' for all of them.

For example, only 58 per cent of children are vaccinated against measles in this country compared to 100 per cent in America.

TREATS

Unchanged for fifty years is the idea of best treat – for the average child it's still a day out, ideally at the seaside. Being taken swimming, fishing or to play tennis all vie for second spot.

One in eight children favours going out for a meal and does so, on average, once every eight weeks. Twenty years ago children eating out were not even a blip on the social behaviour graph – now children's menus are often longer than their parents'.

CHILDREN'S LEISURE

In the swim

What the average child likes doing when he or she has nothing to do, is swimming. It is the most popular sport with all children.

A list of other sports vie for second place. For 20 per cent, 'collecting things' is the favourite hobby. A further 20 per cent put listening to or playing music first.

Parents reckon they spend an average of £58 a year on each child's favourite leisure interest.

AVERAGE VALUE OF BIRTHDAY PRESENTS

The average sum spent by parents on children's birthday presents is £28.60. This is a truly national average with no differences between north, south, boys or girls. Presents themselves are usually clothes and toys, secondly money and cassette players/radios.

The average present bought by children for their friends costs £2.60 – but it is estimated that £2.50 of this, if not more, is parent-sponsored.

AVERAGE REASON FOR SAVING

Rainy days start early

Have we instilled in our children a sense of the impermanence of life – the feeling of apocalypse now or at least very shortly? Seemingly not. The average child, six in ten in fact, saves 'for the future'! Admittedly this statement is rather parent-guided. Left to their own devices half the children would forget the future and spend the money on outings and toys.

AVERAGE TELEVISION VIEWING

Children boxing – not so clever

However much television children watch, almost unanimously parents think it is too much. The average viewing figure is about 19½ hours per week – 2½ hours weekdays, 3½ hours Saturday and Sunday.

Still, one in three parents allow a TV in the child's room. One in six a colour set.

Parents think that TV has a more important influence on boys' tastes and expectations, than girls'. One in two parents stop children watching particular programmes and are stricter with girls than boys.

MINI MCP'S

Chauvinist pigs start young. The average child thinks a woman's role is to stay at home and a man's to go out and work. Boy and girl children shown a TV programme of a knight dashing about on a horse thought his wife would be in the castle – tidying up or doing the dishes.

It is suggested that adult television is much to blame for these stereotyped images – even if unseen, like Arthur Daley's 'her indoors'.

CHILD PUNISHMENT

Taking up the smack

The good old smack lives on. The average parent agrees with Bernard Shaw's dictum, only hit a child in anger, and delivers such an admonishment when necessary.

One in five parents withhold a promised treat; one in seven withhold pocket money; one in twenty withdraw viewing rights on the television.

AVERAGE POCKET MONEY

The pound in your pocket has been devalued!

The average per week per child is 109p. It's bad news for children. Pocket money is just not keeping pace with inflation – it's down 14 per cent on last year.

Outside earnings, however, at 44p are a massive 57 per cent up on the previous year. This extra income is needed to countermand the disappointing drop in handouts from relatives. Only in Scotland and the North is there an overall increase in income which is primarily due to relative generosity.

No one can say British children don't need the money – if only to maintain the national standard of being the world's biggest consumer of sweets. And the statistic which must make the chololate bar and sweet manufacturer drool is the massive £18.2 million children have to spend – weekly!

AVERAGE BOOK

What's the reading matter?

Enid Blyton and the *Beano* are the favourite reading of eleven-year-olds of both sexes. While girls outnumber boys in naming Miss Blyton, both love the Famous Five books because 'they're funny, adventurous, never boring and always end happily' and they are without 'enormous' words. Some think, though, that the heroes get out of trouble too easily.

Other popular authors are Roald Dahl, *(Charlie and the Chocolate Factory)*, C. S. Lewis *(The Lion the Witch and the Wardrobe)*, Richard Adams *(Watership Down)*, Anna Sewell *(Black Beauty)* and Johanna Spyri *(Heidi)*.

Half the children would rather read a book than a comic.

Beano is the runaway favourite comic – particularly with boys, who like its humour, plots and characters.

The bedroom is the favourite place for reading.

Unlike fifteen-year-olds, eleven-year-olds prefer fiction to fact. A third said they preferred reading to watching telly. More girls prefer reading to telly watching. A quarter of both sexes prefer telly.

Myself, I prefer something a little lighter than documentary and true-life drama.

Not still at that stage are you, son?

BREAKFAST TIME

The kids are having takeaway service.

FAMILY DECISIONS

What d'you think kid?

The average child is very much seen and heard when family decisions are made. Even when choosing where to go on holiday or the next car, 6 in 10 parents say they use child consultancy.

ADOLESCENT ENDS

The average young person between 15 and 21 thinks he or she will die of old age. It's encouraging that youth of any generation have the same belief in their immortality – 'old age' is an eternity away.

Twenty per cent think war will kill them or maybe disease . . .

A.M. starts early down south

Parents in the north should shout up the stairs at their young sloths if they're not up by 7am. The average child in the south-east is up by this time; only 1 in 10 needs a 'lot of persuasion'.

It is to be hoped that your children are among that small 6 per cent who have a bath or shower. 1 child in 3 joins the Great Unwashed – neither washing nor teeth cleaning.

Breakfast is no longer a family thing. Only 1 in 8 children eats it with the rest of the family. And breakfast itself, if it is more than just a drink, will be a cereal – probably with a little breakfast telly. Porridge is a rare delight – and even rarer in Scotland.

Ulster children fare best of all. They usually have breakfast served to them and whereas most UK children have some morning chore to do, the average Ulster child does nothing at all at all.

GIRLFRIENDS AND BOYFRIENDS
Go-steady ready

The average teenager is not going out with anybody of the opposite sex. Fewer than 40 per cent have a 'steady' girl or boyfriend. 20 per cent never go out with anyone.

SELF IMAGE

I think I'm . . .

The average teenager thinks of him/her self as friendly, responsible, happy and helpful.

Only 14 per cent would describe themselves as worried. Only 14 per cent would admit to being sometimes violent – although among West Indian males the percentage rises to 35 per cent. But then far more of them are unemployed.

Who's a pretty boy then?

I'm sorry Mr Jessop, but I can't let you have your urine sample to throw at a policeman.

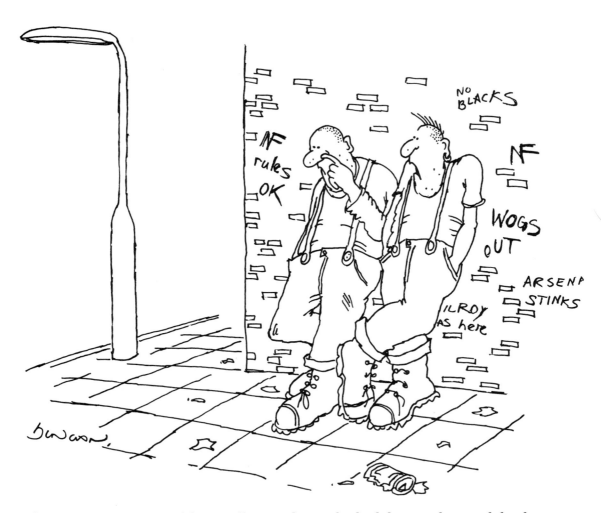

Oh, pretty average sort of day, really. You know, kicked the cat, slammed the door, got an earful from the old lady, slammed the door, felt depressed, kicked the cat again, slammed the door . . .

You: As an average child

£70,000! You must be kidding?

The average cost of raising one child to the age of 16 is about £70,000.

If you are into quantity, take solace from the fact that each additional child will cost you only an extra £1,000 a year. But if you are into quality as well and educate your child privately, the total soars to well over £100,000.

Most of this huge sum is the loss of the wife's earnings but there is £20,000 of direct outlay on food, presents, holidays, clothes and of course shoes, shoes, shoes. It is the price of these which really angers mothers – who claim that £75 a year can all too easily be swallowed up by five or six pairs for the pre-school child.

Baby's first year costs only 8 per cent of its parents' income. By the time the child reaches 16 the cost has risen to 26 per cent of their income. And if the child stays on at school until 18, the cost rises like Concorde – swiftly and steeply.

Although having children is more expensive than 50 per cent of parents expect, only 3 per cent see no advantage in having children in the first place. They give considerable pleasure and improve family life is the popular opinion. The little darlings.

YOU: As an average adult

INTELLIGENCE QUOTIENT

The average man has a brain 10 per cent larger than the average woman. But woman's is larger in comparison to her overall size.

An Intelligence Quotient of 100 means you are of average intelligence so when you learn that the UK national average for man and woman is 100 it must mean we're right on target.

Well it sort of does, but it seems that some other countries are getting cleverer – or maybe just getting better at taking the tests. The Japanese for instance have a national IQ level of 106.

HEIGHT

Walking not so tall

No wonder we have so many proverbs of the 'good things come in small parcels' variety; we are not a tall race.

The average height of an adult woman is 5ft 3½ins (160.9cm) and for a man, 5ft 8½ins (173.3cm).

If at this moment you are a girl of 16½ and hoping to be taller, you may well be. On average you are 98 per cent of your final height which means you've probably another 1½ inches to go. Boys are 98 per cent of their final height at 17¾.

It is worth young girls aspiring to average height and above if they wish to be 'upwardly mobile'. It has been established that taller women tend to marry into a higher social class; shorter-than-average women are unlikely to.

THE AVERAGE WEIGHT

Wait for it . . .

To be average you must weigh, nude, 11st 8lb (73.6kg) if male; 9st 11lb (62.0kg) if female.

Obviously height comes into it and the chart below gives average weight relative to height.

As a nation flesh pots are our downfall – we have too many of them. Nearly 40 per cent of all males and 32 per cent of all females should lose a jam-jar or two of the water, iron, calcium and other bits which go to make up what we loosely call flesh.

Of slim solace to ageing man could be that while women, on average, get fattish and then fatter and fatter, men tend to halt in middle age so that the 50–64 year old man is somewhat lighter than at 40–49 years.

It's as if Time, fed-up with doing the nasty things – like shortening our breath, hardening our hearing and thinning our hair, just temporarily gives us a break – before getting on with the wrinkling and artery hardening.

WOMEN – AVERAGE HEIGHT/WEIGHT

Age Group	Height	Average Weight	Age Group	Height	Average Weight
16–19	up to 5′	8st 0¾lb (51.1kg)		5′ 5″	10st 0¾lb (63.9kg)
	5′ 1″ (155.0cm)	8st 1lb (51.2kg)		5′ 7″	10st 2½lb (64.7kg)
	5′ 3″ (160.0cm)	8st 12¼lb (56.4kg)		over 5′ 7″	10st 12lb (69.0kg)
	5′ 5″ (165.0cm)	9st 6¼lb (60.0kg)	40–49	up to 5′	9st 0½lb (57.4kg)
	5′ 7″ (170.0cm)	9st 13¾lb (63.2kg)		5′ 1″	9st 6¼lb (60.0kg)
	over 5′ 7″	9st 13½lb (63.3kg)		5′ 3″	9st 12¼lb (62.7kg)
20–29	up to 5′	8st 5½lb (53.3kg)		5′ 5″	10st 8½lb (67.3kg)
	5′ 1″	8st 11¾lb (56.1kg)		5′ 7″	10st 9¼lb (67.7kg)
	5′ 3″	9st 3¾lb (58.8kg)		over 5′ 7″	11st 8lb (73.5kg)
	5′ 5″	9st 9lb (61.3kg)	50–64	up to 5′	9st 1¾lb (58.0kg)
	5′ 7″	9st 12lb (62.6kg)		5′ 1″	9st 10¾lb (62.0kg)
	over 5′ 7″	10st 6¼lb (66.3kg)		5′ 3″	10st 4lb (65.3kg)
30–39	up to 5′	8st 8½lb (54.7kg)		5′ 5″	10st 9½lb (67.8kg)
	5′ 1″	9st 0¼lb (57.2kg)		5′ 7″	11st (69.9kg)
	5′ 3″	9st 9lb (61.3kg)		over 5′ 7″	11st 6¼lb (72.7kg)

MEN – AVERAGE HEIGHT/WEIGHT

Age Group	Height	Average Weight	Age Group	Height	Average Weight
16–19	up to 5′ 5½″	9st 5lb (59.5kg)		5′ 10″	12st 21lb (77.2kg)
	5′ 6″ (168.0cm)	9st 5½lb (59.7kg)		6′	12st 8¼lb (80.0kg)
	5′ 8″ (173.0cm)	10st (63.5kg)		over 6′	13st 0¾lb (82.9kg)
	5′ 10″ (178.0cm)	10st 10¼lb (68.2kg)	40–49	up to 5′ 5½″	10st 7¼lb (66.8kg)
	6′ (190.0cm)	11st 3½lb (71.4kg)		5′ 6″	11st 6lb (72.7kg)
	over 6′	11st 3¾lb (71.5kg)		5′ 8″	11st 13½lb (76.0kg)
20–29	up to 5′ 5½″	9st 8¼lb (60.9kg)		5′ 10″	12st 8lb (79.8kg)
	5′ 6″	10st 9½lb (67.8kg)		6′	13st 2lb (83.7kg)
	5′ 8″	11st (69.9kg)		over 6′	13st 9¾lb (87.0kg)
	5′ 10″	11st 10lb (74.4kg)	50–64	up to 5′ 5½″	10st 3¾lb (65.2kg)
	6′	11st 13lb (75.7kg)		5′ 6″	11st 4¼lb (71.9kg)
	over 6′	12st 6¼lb (79.1kg)		5′ 8″	11st 11½lb (75.1kg)
30–39	up to 5′ 5½″	10st 1lb (64.0kg)		5′ 10″	12st 6¼lb (79.1kg)
	5′ 6″	10st 13¾lb (69.7kg)		6′	13st 0¾lb (82.9kg)
	5′ 8″	11st 9¾lb (74.3kg)		over 6′	13st 11lb (87.5kg)

You're just about average for your age and overweight.
High blood pressure and hardening arteries.

Heavier and taller yet

The average height and weight increases with each generation. In 1785 the average man's height was 5ft 4in and weight 9st 4lb.

Captain Bligh was 5ft 4in – the 25 mutineers looked down on him from their average height of 5ft 5in. Nelson was 5ft 2½in and never weighed more than 6 stones as an adult (perhaps the average arm and eye weigh more than we realise). Evidence is scantier for women but they are thought to have averaged 4ft 11½in.

Dem bones

Bone growth is continuous – in the average lifetime, the whole skeleton is replaced 30 times.

Fleshing it out

The average adult body contains enough carbon to make 9,000 pencils, enough phosphorus to make 2,000 match heads, enough fat to make 7 bars of soap and enough iron to make a big nail.

Heady stuff

The brain uses a quarter of the body's oxygen supply. The average air intake a day is about 16,000 litres – which is equivalent to blowing up a balloon the size of the average kitchen, every day.

My own personal little miracle is that after all that I'm still 90% water.

YOUR AVERAGE BODY

Your good health

No milkman would take on the job if your heart took daily delivery of its blood supply in bottles. It's not just a few *crates* even. The average adult heart pumps 8000 pints of blood around your body daily, which means that your 8 pints circulate 1000 times a day.

LENGTH

O.K. chaps, this is where you hold your breath. The average length in its erect state is 6½ inches.

That wasn't so bad was it? Now breathe easy. Researches reveal that no matter how often accepted sexual authorities tell us that it doesn't matter how long it is, we don't believe them.

Most men would happily settle for the next size up. Scott Fitzgerald thought a lot about it. Apparently, his friend Ernest Hemingway told him not to worry — everything looks smaller when you look down on it.

Although man can, with justification, claim to be the biggest primate in this respect (gorillas have been misrepresented), he is a non-starter compared to many animals. The average horse for instance will modestly sport eighteen inches. But for complex-giving of the inferiority kind, consider the whelk. Elevated to human size, the whelk would have a winkle 8ft long.

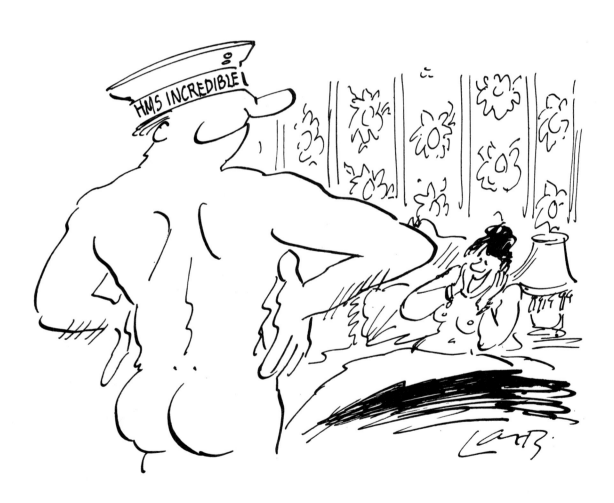

BUSTS

Abreast of the times

Busts are bursting out – the average is now 36″. Only a decade or so ago the most popular bra size was 34″ in a modest B cup.

Now we are catching up with the Italians and the Americans – the Danes are still way in front with 60 in every 100 bras a D cup. In the UK 1 in 5 is 40″ or more in a D cup.

An indication that things may be getting out of hand is that 1 in 8 women would like to lose weight from this generally admired area.

WAISTS

The average is 29″ and 7 in 10 women would like to waste away between 1 and 4 inches.

HIPS

– no hooray

The average is 39″ and it is here that women find it all too much, flesh wise: 9 in 10 would like to lose 3 inches. The average woman wishes she was 35″ 25″ 36″ and weighed 8st 12lb – a full 13lb lighter than reality.

The most sought after figure is one like Felicity Kendal's who is rated above Victoria Principal, Bo Derek, Raquel Welch and the Princess of Wales.

The Venus de Milo's well-rounded look is out. She, in the flesh, would have weighed in at well over 11st.

Now just wait right there, Mr Hobson,
I'm sure there's another midget here somewhere.

That's torn it David – here comes his Dad.

You weigh eight stone seven-and-a-half pounds and we have to stop meeting like this, Shirley, I'm getting cramp again.

I had no idea there had been any EEC directives for the standardisation of bust and hip measurements.

DIET

The average woman diets and has probably been doing so since she was aged 20 – 1 in 4 women start at 15. Many women get depressed if they are not dieting; it is part of their way of life, particularly for those under 35.

On average they weigh themselves once a week to check progress (if any) and 1 in 4 weighs daily.

3 in 4 women think they are overweight, 1 in 5 thinks she is very overweight. Only 1 in 20 thinks she is just right and diets to stay that way.

REASONS FOR DIETING
It was just one of those thins

Although the average woman thinks the average man likes slim figures and she herself envies slimmer women, she slims for her own satisfaction – thinking she will look and feel better, be healthier and live longer. 2 in 3 women think it would improve their personalities to be slimmer.

Men are just as concerned about being overweight as women but only half as many do anything about it. Men rarely take up any keep fit or yoga exercises and their fitness routine is confined to their irregular sporting activities.

Overall though, men are in better shape. Fifty years ago the waist of Edwardian man was only about 2 inches smaller than his chest. Now, the shape we generally call 'manly' is much more pronounced and there is likely to be 4–5 inches difference between waist and chest measurements.

I wish I weighed enough to start dieting.

NO EXERCISE
A leotard can't change your pots

25 per cent of women never exercise, although 60 per cent of them own a leotard – the same percentage as own a tracksuit.

NO SURGERY
Cut it out!

Fewer than 1 in 50 women contemplete this solution, bodily or facially, to their weight problem but interest is growing. In the States, 4 in ever 10 cosmetic operations are on men. Male statistics here don't even register.

OVERWEIGHT EXAM
Fat, Fatter, Fat Test

Use this simple test to see if you are overweight. Multiply your height by itself and divide this figure into your weight. This is what the sum looks like:

$$\frac{\text{Your weight (in kilogrammes)}}{\text{Your height} \times \text{your height (in metres)}} = \text{less than 25, you hope}$$

Example

You are 5′ 5″ tall and weigh 10st 2½lb
5′ 5″ is 1.65 metres: 10st 2½lb is 64.7kg

So $\frac{64.7}{1.6 \times 1.6} = 23.76$ You're in good shape

If the total is over 25 you are averagely overweight. If the figure reaches 30 or above you'd have to be described as really OBE – and the rest.

TO SLEEP

with thanks and acknowledgements to
Roger Hargreaves and Paul Sellers

A man sleeps an average of 8 hours a night; a woman, 8 hours 20 minutes. Most women feel they need more sleep than a man but even though they get it, 58 per cent agree, a man is brighter in the mornings.

The average man snores — which could have an effect on the quality of his partner's sleep. The average woman doesn't. Unless the men are just being chivalrous — or sleep too heavily to notice.

THE AVERAGE DREAM?

Most people dream even if they have no memory of it afterwards. The average dream-span is 1¾ hours in five separate periods. Whatever the real interpretation of dreams, they are slimming stuff; the average adult loses 1lb (½kg) while asleep.

Damn! I had a marvellous dream, and I can't remember a thing about it.

FEET

The average pair will walk 150,000 miles in a lifetime. In view of this it's amazing how few of us put a foot wrong. Only 3–4 per cent of the population ever go to a chiropodist – until . . . you are sixty-five years old. If you visit one then you'll be on equal footing with nearly two million others of your age group.

DOCTOR VISITS

Do you seem to be in the doctor's surgery much more often than your neighbours, family and friends? Don't worry. They are probably not as average as you.

The average man visits the doctor twice a year, the average woman three or four times a year. Up to age sixteen, it is four times a year for both sexes.

An overwhelming majority of us try to choose a doctor of our own sex – older men in particular are 'resistant' to women doctors.

The doctor's time with you is short. On average a doctor will spend twenty hours a week seeing patients; less than in doing all that admin – telephone work, letters, practice discussions, meetings and reading – and thinking, no doubt.

The average GP has a patient list of over 2,000. Obviously, responsibility for the health of such a legion is highly stressful and doctors get more than averagely depressed. The incidence of wife-bashing is the highest of all the professions. It is not recorded whether the 20 per cent of doctors who are female hit their husbands.

The average prescription, as well as being illegible, costs £4.50.

I would strongly advise you to give up smoking or you won't be able to afford my bill.

OPTICIANS

A popular spectacle

Men are seriously limiting their social lives if they seldom make passes at girls who wear glasses, as Dorothy Parker suggested. The average adult man and adult woman wears glasses.

Six million pairs are dispensed every year. The use of contact lenses is growing but the total number is still under one million – 7 in every 10 users are women.

OK, OK. Try the second line.

. . . What's more not one of us wears contact lenses — and we're all football referees!

JAWS

It takes 50 per cent more force to keep an average man's mouth shut than an average woman's.

Using a specially designed extra-oral gnathodynamometer to clamp jaws shut, four Glasgow dentists measured the force exerted by men and women to open their mouths. Apparently neither age nor size has much bearing on the results.

TEETH CLEANING

The average man and woman clean their teeth for only 20 seconds. Dentists say it is not long enough to avoid caries and gum disorders. 2½ minutes is the recommended time.

DENTISTS

The average adult doesn't mind going to the dentist – fewer than 2 in 5 are now 'apprehensive'. It seems the time and effort dentists have put into improving their image has paid off.

It must be time to work on their own self-image. They are the most depressed of professions, despite the good money – dental principals earn on average £42,000 pa.

The average number of visits to the dentist is two a year; the average number of fillings in the average mouth is six. The average cost of treatment is £15.50.

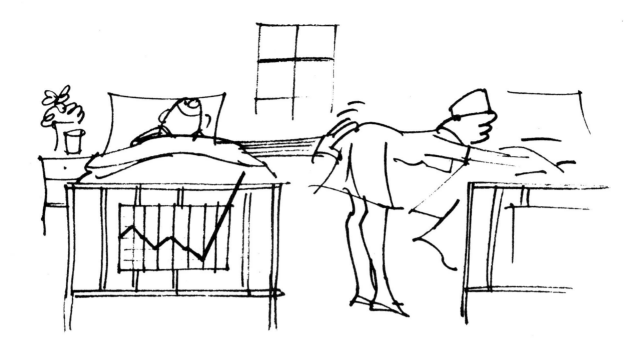

NATIONAL HEALTH SERVICE

Hospitable life

The average person thinks the NHS a good service.

In-patients praise nurses and medical care and think only the food below average acceptability. Out-patients, and 3 in 4 of us have been hospital out-patients, are completely satisfied with their treatment.

Impatience is caused only by the appointment system which still keeps one patient in three waiting a 'very long time' to see a doctor or specialist.

I'm sorry Mrs Hislop, we had to destroy your husband in order to save him.

AVERAGE PRIVATE PATIENT SUBSCRIPTION

Over 4 million people are in private medical schemes with the average reason given – to avoid the dreaded National Health waiting list. The average private plan subscription is £160 per annum. Most schemes are run by companies, only a quarter are paid by private individuals.

Private schemes are reckoned to deal with 37,500 patients a day.

I'll have to give you a referral.
We're only equipped to deal with cases of up to £1000 here.

SUICIDE

We're a reasonably cheerful lot in the UK — better than most countries anyway. We average 8 suicides per 100,000 population, that is a daily average of 13 people.

The EEC average at 12 in 100,000 is the same as the USA with the exception of San Francisco which often achieves a figure of 2,000 in 100,000, that is 1 person in 50.

In Europe generally suicide is less common in strongly Catholic/Orthodox countries even taking into account possible statistical blurring by an unnaturally high rate of 'accidents'. The worst countries in Europe are Austria, Hungary and Finland. The fewest suicides occur in Ireland, Iceland and Greece.

In the UK on average there are 15 attempts for every successful suicide. Most suicides occur in the autumn. 6 in 10 are men, who are most likely to hang themselves or use gas, often the car exhaust. Women most often take a drug overdose.

The magic's gone out of my marriage, my Volvo and my home computer.

SOS

Fighting the problem in this country are 20,000 Samaritans, who answer 328,000 calls for help each year.

AVERAGE LENGTH OF LIFE

With all the scientific progress and growth of medical knowledge it's odd that man is still struggling to achieve his allotted lifespan, laid down by God some 5000 years ago.

Most men die in their 69th year. Women sail easily past the finishing line with an average 75.6 years, which is about the same total lifespan and ratio between the sexes as America. If you want to live longest you should be Japanese, who average 74.5 for men and 80.2 years for women.

UK children born now will fare much better than their parents – an average lifespan of 77 for men is estimated and for women, well over 80. An average lifespan of between 85 and 90 is predicted for those born in the next decade.

Look on the bright side, dear – when Mozart was your age he'd been dead fifteen years . . .

AVERAGE DEATH

I don't mind dying, I just don't want to be there when it happens. – Woody Allen

The average person dies of a heart attack. Just over half of all deaths, 51.9 per cent, are due to a coronary thrombosis. Scotland and Ireland have the dubious honour of leading the world in deaths from heart attacks with 300 deaths per 100,000 citizens.

If this way of demise is particularly abhorrent to you – and it can be argued, what method isn't? – you must go to France where only 38 per cent die of heart attacks.

But then up go your chances of death from disgestive complaints, cirrhosis, ulcers, etc. The liver becomes a real misnomer. Deaths in France from its malfunction are twice those in the UK. And doesn't Ireland, to be sure, have the lowest rating in the world from cirrhosis deaths: a mere 4.7 deaths per 100,000 people.

You have a 1 in 4 chance of dying from cancer. Scotland, then England/Wales, are respectively third and fourth in the league of deaths from carcinomic causes, and unfortunately lead the world in deaths from lung cancer.

A mere 4 per cent die from accident, poison and violence.

50

Yes – there's a lot of it about.

You know what I regret? Losing the will to live.

He was a dreadful hypochondriac.

LATE PRICES

*Ah well then, I suppose I shall have to die
beyond my means* – Oscar Wilde

As the cost of living rises so does the cost of
dying – it's galloping expiration.

The average funeral costs between £300 and
£600.

The Welsh Consumer Council, who no
doubt know what it means to Dai, has called
for a £250 grant to replace the £30 one, where
a deceased person's estate is less than £5,000.

You and your family

YOU AS A NATIONAL FIGURE

Firstly, let's put the average you into national perspective. You are one of 56 million inhabitants of the United Kingdom – which is England, Scotland, Wales and Northern Ireland. (Great Britain does not include Northern Ireland.)

You will be nestling somewhere among the 34 million people of working age, probably. They form 60 per cent of the country's population. There are also 12 million children and 10 million elderly.

YOU AS A HOUSEHOLD

Whether you live alone or have a large family you will be considered a household. There are 21 million in the UK with an ethnic breakdown as follows:

Place of Birth	Percentage of Population
UK	93.0
Irish Republic	1.6
Caribbean	0.8
Indian	0.9
Pakistan/Bangladesh	0.4
Other New Commonwealth	1.0
Others	2.3

93% white . . .

53

AVERAGE HOUSEHOLD

The number of people living in the average household is 2.64. When you first read this you may wonder if one little 0.64 of a person could meet another 0.64, have a couple of baby 0.32's and have a go at being a whole family It doesn't work like that.

A UK average household size of 2.64 people means there are a lot of people living alone and a lot of two-person families. These balance the much smaller number of households with six, seven, eight or more people, to give the national average of 2.64.

There are over 5 million people living by themselves in the UK. 67 per cent of them are women – primarily because they so consistently outrun their partners in the longevity stakes. Greater London has the highest proportion of people living alone – 26 per cent of its population.

One-parent families have risen to 2.38 million to represent 11.5 per cent of all households. Over one-third of all households are two-person households.

Merseyside has the highest proportion of households with five or more people – outside Ireland that is, where nearly one-third of all households have five or more people.

There is an average of 7.3 people in households where the head is of non-UK birth.

The time-honoured notion of the typical family being a married couple with two children now exists primarily on ageing admen's storyboards. Only 12 per cent of UK families are the classic 2+2, although four in five people think this is the average family .

MARITAL STATUS

He is dreadfully married. He's the most married man I ever saw in my life. – Artemus Ward

The average person is married. The chart shows just how married:

	Single	Married	Widowed	Divorced
Men	27.6	65.7	3.7	3.1
Women	21.0	60.7	14.4	3.9
Percentage of Population	24.2	63.0	9.2	3.5

NUMBER OF CHILDREN

Statistically a family begins at two people. By this definition three in four households are families.

The average family has 0.8 children.

This means the UK population is not even replacing itself. For the last thirteen years there has been a decline. It last happened in the 20s and 30s but even in the aftermath of the wars women 'completed their families later'.

An average family size of 2.1 children is needed if we are to keep a steady population of young people. The population for example of England and Wales has grown by only 0.4 per cent over the last ten years.

Part of the reason for our lack of procreation is the efficiency of contraceptive methods which allow accurate family planning and the increasing number who opt for sterilisation. In 1 in 5 couples under 44 one partner is sterilised. Between 35 and 44 the percentage goes up to 4 in 10.

Is he one of ours?

with thanks and acknowledgements to the *Daily Mail*

Mother's here, George. Will you go and help her with her things?

MOTHERS-IN-LAW

The average couple like their mothers-in-law.

They always did. Even before they tied the knot, over half the married population liked their prospective mothers-in-law at first meeting. In Scotland 2 out of 3 describe their relationship as fabulous – which is about as un-dour as you can get.

Women get on better with their mothers-in-law, on average, than men do, but only marginally so – an Ashford, Kent man recently married his.

Least liked are the mothers of only sons.

GRANDPARENTS

The average age at which parents become grandparents is now 47.

THE AVERAGE HOME

The average home is a house – beating flats into second place by four to one. A third are terraced, a third semi-detached, the remaining third split equally between detached, bungalows and the ubiquitous 'others'.

Most of us own our own homes:

	UK Generally	Scotland Only
Owner	61%	37%
Rent:		
Local Authority	28%	53%
Private	11%	10%

This could be bloody serious –
suppose he applies for a council house.

Currently more Scots live in council houses than any other group in the UK. But exhibiting the canniness for which they are famed, their mortgage applications are the highest in the country. We cannot confirm the truth of the story of the Scot at the Sassenach Building Society who asked for a wee house being directed to the public convenience.

It is reckoned that by AD 2000 75 per cent of all homes will be owner-occupied, less than 20 per cent will be council housing, the rest privately rented.

NEW HOUSE PRICE

The average new house costs £28,738 to buy.

First-time buyers spend an average of £21,918; others £36,233.

The average house prices have gone up over the last fifteen years at a rate only slightly more than the income of borrowers. But it is the doubling of the mortgage interest rates that has kept buyers stretched.

House prices are 31 per cent above the average in London, and anywhere in the south is 10 per cent above the national norm. Northern Ireland is the cheapest place to buy a house at 27 per cent below average.

The average couple buying a new home will buy a house. More detached houses are currently being built than bungalows, flats or

maisonettes. Semi-d's are the next most popular homes with terraced houses, flats and maisonettes together forming about 20 per cent of the total residential building scene.

The average mortgage is 85 per cent of the total price for first-time buyers; for others it averages just under 60 per cent. The average income of a first-time borrower is under £10,000; average income of others over £11,500.

The average new house buyer is dissatisfied in some major respect. One in eight new houses is described as 'terrible'. Only one in eight is described as fault-free.

AVERAGE HOME VALUE
Prices through the roof

Terraced house: £23,700
Flat: £25,400
Semi-detached: £29,200
Bungalow: £35,500
Detached: £47,300

These prices add up to an overall average value of a home of £31,300. In London figures can be 3 or 4 times the national average. Pockets in the south-west and Scotland are also likely to be double the average value.

HOW WE SPEND OUR MONEY

with thanks and acknowledgements to *The Sunday Times* 6.1.85

AVERAGE HOUSEHOLD SPEND

Let us be happy and live within our means even if we have to borrow the money to do so. — Artemus Ward

Every week the average household spends about £150. You as an average person spend about £56.

These figures are for the middle income group. In the low income group where the head of household is out of work, or in two-person pensioner households, weekly spending is about half the average and most of it goes on fuel, food and housing.

In the high income group – households where both man and woman work – the weekly spend is about £200. This is nearly 25 per cent higher than if the woman is a housewife.

Household spending varies greatly from region to region too. In the north expenditure is about 14 per cent below the average and in

AVERAGE WEEKLY SHOPPING

How much did you say you'd spent?

Woman shopping for the average household say they spend £25.73 on food every week and a 'complete family shop' including food costs £38.58.

Two in ten men have no idea how much of the family income goes on food – even though four out of ten actually help with the weekly shop. Most of them don't mind and 17 per cent positively enjoy it.

AVERAGE SHOPPING PLACE

Buying Big

The average woman favours a big supermarket for her weekly shop. Only 10 per cent shop elsewhere. Specialist shops are most popular in Scotland where six in ten prefer the personal service. In the Midlands one in five women does a regular shop in a health-food shop.

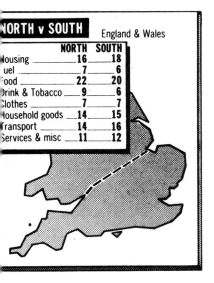

NORTH v SOUTH	England & Wales	
	NORTH	SOUTH
Housing	16	18
Fuel	7	6
Food	22	20
Drink & Tobacco	9	6
Clothes	7	7
Household goods	14	15
Transport	14	16
Services & misc	11	12

the south about the same percentage above.

Figuratively speaking, though, we all put a lot of money where our mouth is – in all categories, food takes the most money and highest percentage of weekly income.

Only the Italians and Greeks spend more: the Italians spend more than a quarter of their weekly incomes on food; the Greeks more than a third.

AVERAGE FOOD SPEND

I eat merely to put food out of my mind. –
N F Simpson

The average person spends £11 a week on food. This is the average shopping list:

Just can't resist a special offer, dear.

Avoiding health foods has added an
undeniable challenge to our lives.

Milk – down to an average of just under 4 pints a week. Partially due to a decline in tea drinking.

Sugar – up to 10½oz despite universal condemnation. It's one of the things we are all trying to give up.

Eggs – down to an average of 3½ per week. Half an egg less than 5 years ago but still half an egg more than medical recommendation for cholesterol levels.

Meat – down to 12oz a week. We're eating about the same amount of beef but less pork and lamb – except in Ireland which eats twice the national beef average.

Poultry – up ½lb a week.

Fish – unchanged consumption. Mancunians eat a lot more fish and brown bread and salads than the rest of the nation.

Potatoes – for each person it's down to under 3lb a week with the Welsh eating much more than that and the English about 2lb per head.

Fresh vegetables – as many reports say we're eating more as say we're eating less. It's probably unchanged

Bread – down to about 2 loaves a week.

Butter – up to 3½oz. The Welsh eat twice the national average.

Cheese – down to under 4oz per head.

If you have an eye for averageness in the future, you'll be looking to reduce your meat, sugar, salt and butter intake.

There is a 60 per cent increase in the shift towards the vegetarian diet. The reasons given are coronary concerns, domestic economics and the ethics of killing the 500 million animals we eat a year.

The average person in a life-time consumes 140,000lb of food – equivalent to eating an average-sized rhinoceros every year.

AVERAGE HOUSEHOLD DUTIES

You would think that with the increase in the number of working women and the decline in work available our domestic lives would have changed dramatically, wouldn't you? But . . .

The woman in the average household does almost all the housework. It doesn't matter if she is at home all day, works part-time or has a full-time job, a woman's work is never done – not by a man it's not.

It's not as if the average woman likes housework. Ironing is positively disliked by 99 per cent of all women; and like nature, most women abhor a vacuum – hoovering is the next most disliked job. Washing up seems to give a warm glow to only 25 per cent. Men, perhaps feeling a bit guilty, think they, and claim to, 'help a lot'. Some even say they do 40 per cent of all housework. Women disagree. For instance, 20 per cent of men claim that they help with the ironing. Women say only 1 or 2 per cent of men know where the board is kept. It's the same with other domestic labours.

Men: Slothaholics Synonymous

Mowing the lawn – only 40 per cent of men do it. Home decorating – only 30 per cent of men do it. Odd jobs – only 33 per cent of men do them. General repairs is the only area in which men achieve domestic equality. Such tasks are usually split 50–50. The one area in which men and women agree on how much a man does is 'looking after the children'. Presumably depending on the family setup, this can be considered a chore or a pleasure but 20 per cent is done by men. A percentage agreed by both.

It seems that to be sure of being a truly average male today – don't do anything about the house. Jerome K Jerome's observation on how much he liked work – he 'could watch it for hours', seems to have been taken as a commandment by men domestically.

AVERAGE TIME IN KITCHEN

The average British housewife spends between 7–10 hours a week preparing meals – about 1½ hours a day.

In the Midlands and Wales they spend an extra two hours a week on average and in the north-east and London two hours less.

AVERAGE TIME ON SHOPPING

Four hours a week. Except in Glasgow where 20 per cent say they spend up to ten hours a week.

Good God is that the time? That's ten hours I've been slaving in this kitchen today.

HOME TELEPHONE

Call me expensive

Average yearly telephone charges are £133 including rental.

The average call is three minutes – yes, only three minutes. You have to be disciplined to be average. 92 per cent of all home calls are local – even 83 per cent of business calls are local.

The number of outgoing calls per telephone is 675 a year on average, which is about two a day allowing time out for holidays. We have more telephones – and more televisions for that matter – than any other country in Europe. We have something like 29 million handsets in our 21 million households.

And having got used to the wireless wireless we are now into cordless telephones – they have already captured 5 per cent of the market.

I'm utterly sick of having to admire the contents of his deep freeze.

FIXTURES AND FITTINGS AND APPLIANCES

The average household has:

A television (98 per cent of all households; 17 per cent b & w only)
A bath/shower (97 per cent of all households)
A fridge (94 per cent)
A vacuum cleaner (95 per cent)
Central heating (64 per cent)
A washing machine (79 per cent)
A telephone (77 per cent)
A car (60 per cent)
A deep freeze (51 per cent)
A food mixer (66 per cent)

The average household does not have:

Tumble dryer (in only 27 per cent of households)
Video recorder (33 per cent)
Home computer (25 per cent)
Microwave oven (8 per cent)
Blender/Liquidiser (47 per cent)
Pressure cooker (44 per cent)
Deep fat fryer (25 per cent)
Toasted sandwich maker (44 per cent)
Slow cooker (14 per cent)

Do you realise that we're the only people we know who aren't among the privileged few?

DUSTBINS

Every day 50,000 tons of rubbish are thrown out of our homes.

The average dustbin in a year contains:

enough paper to save six trees
enough food waste to keep a garden in compost
half a ton of glass, metal and plastic
58 per cent of the population would support a tax increase to reduce the current waste of natural resources by recycling glass and paper. Many think it would create jobs and contribute to greater prosperity long term.

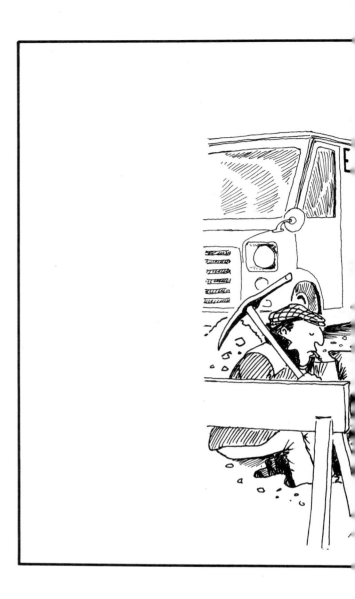

FUEL BILL

These fuelish things . . .

The average fuel bill in the average home is between £450 and £500 per annum. This is for the total of gas, electricity, oil and coal if used.

GAS

End of therm report

Your gas consumption costs you, as the average householder, just under £250 a year.

ELECTRICITY

Watt?

Your electricity consumption – on all those machines and items of equipment in your average house – costs you over £260 a year.

AVERAGE RATE DEMAND

The going rate – which comes too often

The average household pays rates of £275 per annum with a rateable value of £200. London rates are the highest in the country with an average sum payable of £450.

WATER RATE

Based on a household with an average rateable value, the average water rate is £80 – with Anglia the most expensive area, 14 per cent above average, and the north-west the least expensive, 14 per cent below average.

LETTERS

On average you receive 274 letters a year of which just under half are private or social – plus 5 letters from overseas and 4 parcels.

Of the non-social items, 37 are bills and 28 statements, receipts and such like.

The principal people in your postal bombardment are: manufacturers who send an average of 26 items; credit card companies, 21 items; the government and British Telecom, 28 items.

On average 1 in 10 letters arrives late.

It's a miracle I wasn't killed when he tried to
fling his crutches away.

AVERAGE DOMESTIC ACCIDENT

Oooops More Fall You

You are more likely to have an accident in the
home than at work or driving your car.

The average domestic accident is a fall.
There is a lot of falling about – on the level
too, most often in the kitchen or living room.

Stairs are the second most popular tumblers
– with as many people tripping up on the way
down as falling down on the way up.

If you haven't enjoyed such a trip you're
most likely to cut yourself – it's the second
most common domestic accident. If it's a tin
you've cut yourself on, chances are it's a
corned beef tin. Three in every five tin-open-
ing accidents occur trying to entice that trun-
cated pyramid of beef out of its shell.

Life is rather like a tin of corned beef, or
sardines, Alan Bennett has said – we're all of
us looking for the key. Perhaps in the interest
of safety we should give up the search.

We're afraid it's women and children first as far as accidents are concerned. Children under 5 are particularly vulnerable – they are involved in 27 per cent of all house mishaps. Every day over 300 women fall out of bed and over 200 crash into doors – many of them made of glass.

3 per cent are injured in accidental poisoning. And surely we all feel for the 1.9 per cent of the population who suffer an 'over exertion' accident. It is difficult, isn't it, to know the point at which doing it changes to over-doing it and something has to give.

The French are good at accidents. They have more than any other European country and most other countries too. In EEC countries generally, accidental deaths average 5 per cent of the total number. France has been consistently at 7 per cent per annum for years.

Accidentally, things are getting better in the UK. In the last twenty years deaths by accident have fallen by 29 per cent to just over 12,000 fatalities a year. There is a great seasonal variation with 40 per cent more accidents happening in mid-summer than in December.

AVERAGE FINGER

To test that domestic appliances are as safe as possible, the standards people use a British Standard Finger which they try to poke into things such as plug sockets and hair dryers. This mechanical digit can be wielded to simulate the curious, hostile or over-enthusiastic behaviour of its human counterpart.

DISTANCES FROM SERVICES
How far away?

From your average home you will find you are only 1 mile 380 yards from your doctor. Check out these other average distances:

Bus stop	525 yards
Telephone box	1040 yards (there's a 1 in 2 chance it's not working)
Chemist	1 mile
2nd telephone box	1 mile 280 yards
Sub post office	1 mile 370 yards
Doctor	1 mile 380 yards
Chain store	2 miles
Station	2–2½ miles
Hospital	2–3½ miles
Main post office	4 miles

WORK

WORKING PEOPLE

Heigh Ho Heigh Ho. It's off to . . .

The average person, and most people between the working agespan 16 to 65, has a job. There are 23 million people in employment on any average day. That is, 40 per cent of the population, which means that every working person supports himself/herself plus 1.45 people not working, i.e. children, unemployed, pensioners.

WORKING HOURS

The average person works 40 hours a week: men on average 41.4 hours; women 37.2 hours.

For office workers this time is usually 9.00 am start until 5.00 pm finish with about an hour for lunch. Many say they work 'quite a lot longer' than their official time and that

Clock watching again, Belgrove?

most days they do half-an-hour overtime, which is unpaid. Many confess too to periods of 'floating'; that is, not really concentrating on work but physically there. If there is any justice, the floating and overtime should balance.

The average working day for manual workers is 39 hours plus 4 hours overtime which adds some 14 per cent to their basic income.

The average teacher officially works 41 hours a week at secondary level but reckons on working 50 hours a week.

WORK TRAVEL

Commute, commuter, commutest

The average commuter lives less than one hour from work. If the travel to work is by British Rail, the average fare is £1.65 a day.

EARNINGS

Weakly income

The average weekly income per person in the UK is £190. The average for all men is £212 and for all women £133. The longer working week of the average man doesn't really explain the difference in the weekly earnings (see women at work, page 76).

A common thought about earned income by either sex is that there's not enough of it to go round. There never has been.

Karl Marx's mum reckoned it would have been better for all if he had made a lot of kapital instead of writing it. In *Vanity Fair*, Becky Sharp thought that she could be a good woman on £5,000 a year. This was in 1847, and would be equivalent to £520,000 now. Even today most of us could be good – and bad – with such a sum.

No wonder you're late. You've got the big hand pointing to Mickey Mouse's left ear!

AVERAGE TIME TO EARN MONEY FOR YOURSELF

After first paying the tax man and making a health insurance contribution, the average man starts earning money for himself at 11.30 am.

Things have got steadily worse over the last 30 years as the chart below shows:

1953	9.26
1963	10.00
1973	10.55
1984	11.30

You can see the trend – is the day coming when we'll run out of time and money before we've earned it?

AVERAGE WORKING TIME TO BUY GOODS

One person in household working

	Hrs Mins
1 pint fresh milk	4
125gm tea	7
Large white sliced loaf	8
1 pint beer	12
1 dozen medium eggs	13
500gm butter	19
20 cigarettes	20
100gm instant coffee	22
Cinema admission	34
1 gallon petrol (4★)	35
Weekly average telephone bill	40
1lb rump steak	58
Weekly average gas bill	1.07
Weekly average electricity bill	1.14
1cwt coal	1.31
Long playing record	1.41
1 bottle whisky	2.20
Colour TV licence	14.40
Car tax	27.10

Hmm, drinkable – but a bit pricey at 68 minutes.

The average man is a little better off today than 30 years ago – but not very much. In 1973 he was 40 per cent better off than in 1953, but now he has to work 50 per cent longer than in 1973 to buy the same thing.

Between 1973 and 1983 wages rose by 152 per cent against price increases of 212 per cent.

The greatest increase by far is in tax/insurance contributions. Clothing and shoes have gone up at a much greater rate than the cost of living – so have cars, which were relatively cheap in 1973.

Some things are now much cheaper, relatively. Television and washing machines for example.

Tell them that one about your salary increase, Geoffrey.

EXECUTIVE EARNINGS

Nice work if you can get it . . .

£17,500 a year is the salary of the aspiring (and would-be perspiring if it weren't for the sweet-smelling deodorant used by 1 in 3) executive under 40.

Perks are a 2-litre company car, free petrol, expense account and medical insurance.

At the upper end of the figures which have gone to make up this average is the 1 in 5 who earns more than £25,000.

Executives are difficult to qualify averagely: at the lower level now is the self-styled used-vehicle marketing executive – who used to wallow happily in the title 'second-hand car salesman', while at the top end is the chief executive who is so important that he doesn't have to wear a feathered head-dress to prove it.

Average executive accoutrements are often an extruded aluminium briefcase, a watch accurate to 30 fathoms and a backgammon set playable at 30,000 feet.

And if all this sounds a bit of a man's world, it is. Less than 1 executive in 10 is a woman – other than in the retail trade where 1 in 5 managers is female.

But being an executive has its problems – stress for one. The average executive has a higher stress rating than a politician or doctor (see page 83). Plus there's always the risk of over-egoing it. As Francis Bacon put it, 'That he doeth like the ape, the higher he climbs, the more he shows his arse.'

WOMEN AT WORK

The average woman likes working. 85 per cent state emphatically they are 'satisfied with their job' – a much higher percentage than men.

Woman make up 40 per cent of the total UK work force. Yet 15 years after the Equal Pay Act and 9 years after the Sex Discrimination Act, women, on average, earn only two-thirds as much as men. Only 3 in 10 cases heard under the Sex Discrimination Act rule in favour of the woman plaintiff.

Although 60 per cent of women work – against only 20 per cent in 1954 – they are still making very little impression on the professions. Only 4 per cent of architects are women; only 5 per cent of accountants; only 10 per cent of college lecturers; 11 per cent of solicitors; 14 per cent of dentists – and of engineers a mere 0.5 per cent are female.

Much of the reason is that half of them still consider man should be the money-earner and a woman mainly responsible for running the home and looking after the children.

This 'average opinion' is changing amongst the younger set. For example, in the 65-year-old and older age group, 70 per cent think the man should be the primary bread winner, whereas in the 18–34 year age group, only 30 per cent agree with this.

44 per cent of women expect their careers to suffer when they have children. Married women at the moment contribute only 25 per cent of the household budget on average. Only 17 per cent of women in this country with children under 16 are working full-time.

The average working woman – and there are 9 million in total – works full-time, but the percentage of part-timers is rising fast. During the 80s part-time work has increased by 8 per cent so that now, 4 in every 10 working women are part-timing.

When you've got through to New York, file these for me would you?

Given the figures for extra-marital relations (see page 127) this raises an interesting social speculation – can a part-timer and a two-timer develop a one-to-one relationship?

UK women lead Europe and most of the world in the percentage who work. Quite what the significance of this is is hard to tell – unless of course you want to rocket beyond average womanhood, even to lead your country. Most countries which have, or have had a woman premier have a high percentage of working women.

You've certainly more chance of leading your country here than in Russia or even America where the phrase First Lady just means you're the wife of someone who's made it.

CREDIT CARDS
Money plastically everywhere

Nearly 1 in 3 of all adults has a credit card, and spends about £500 a year with it. These cards are of the bank free-issue type not the high falutin' ones you pay for the privilege of using.

For the fancy gold cards you must be earning £25,000 per annum but the average card holder has an income of £39,000.

WHERE DOES IT GO?

When, as a working man or woman, you have earned an average amount of money, what do do you do with it?

The average working man and working woman puts the earnings into a joint account from which both partners can draw.

1 in 5 men puts his money into a personal account; 1 in 3 working wives do too. 1 in 3 men give their wives all or most of their earnings. 4 in 10 give wives a housekeeping allowance.

In Japan, the land of the rising executive, the average number of men who hand over their complete wages and salaries to their wives is much higher than in the UK.

This is not what we'd expect from the wonderful people who gave us the geisha girl and most of the martial arts. Perhaps the men look on it as delegating responsibility – saying, give a Japaneasy life. Or perhaps the women have a yen to handle money.

WORKING IN SERVICE

Over 90 per cent of us are employees. The average Brit works for someone else.

If that sounds as if we are light in the entrepreneurial and adventurous spirit, we are. But we are only just ahead of America, the land of enterprise and opportunity, in our work force working for someone else. Italy, by contrast, has the highest number of people self-employed, at 20 per cent of the total work force.

TYPE OF WORK

As all the best hostesses are supposed never to ask, 'What is it you actually do?'

The average person, 54 per cent, works in a service industry. We stand and wait – serving that diminishing number who are making, growing, and building things for the rest of us to administer, promote and sell.

EXECUTIVE BRIEFCASE

The average executive doesn't buy his own briefcase – it's a present from his wife or girl-friend.

The real revelation is – the average briefcase does *not* contain a diet lunch in a plastic box! 46 per cent, though, contain a change of vest and pants, which could mean either a high-pressure job or lots of travelling. That 1 in 3 cases contains a clean shirt and alarm clock points to the latter reason.

50 per cent of all exec briefcases are never used for business.

There have been complaints, Simkins – you're waking up on the job.

EXECUTIVE WORKING DAY
And I've been working like a dog

The average British executive works longer hours than almost any other country's. It is often up to 10 hours a day – not including travelling time which adds at least another 2 hours. And he loses out on holidays, too, with only 34 days a year on average compared to the French 40, German 41 and Italian 42.

The 10-hour day is considered de rigueur in smaller companies of 100 employees or less, in larger companies the average drops to 8½ hours a day.

AVERAGE EXECUTIVE TELEPHONE CALLS
You're a phoney

The average executive is 'giving someone a bell' 32 times a day – well 39 times a day in the south, 31 times in the north. Although his most used tool, it often works against him. Over half claim that their efficiency is seriously impaired by returning phonecalls and trying to contact other people.

The third thing which eats into their efficiency is other people's unpunctuality.

The difficult thing to sort out is who these 'other' executives are – presumably when they are asked what wastes their day they'll give the same answers.

AVERAGE EXECUTIVE LUNCH
I'll have a small negotiation to start . . .

The average executive lunch takes 2½ hours. But it is where serious business is done, 33 per cent of executives claim. They entertain clients once a week on average.

Another 30 per cent reckon their lunches are purely social and 20 per cent don't take expense account lunches at all – silly boys!

I'll have the Expansionist Businessman's Lunch.

AVERAGE EXECUTIVE DRINK
I don't mind if I do

The average executive tipple is a wee dram o' the hard stuff. Or rather it would be if it wasn't so large – but Scotch it is. It's the same throughout Europe too, with 68 per cent choosing any whisky as their No 1 alcoholic drink.

The Danes and the Swedes are Europe's most spirited executives, with 85 per cent drinking whisky regularly.

Morning doctor — my wife thinks I'm suffering from stress . . . God, is that the time? — Let me have your views in triplicate — Can I use the phone? — My secretary will do the medical . . . Must rush — Let's have lunch some time . . .

AVERAGE WORKING STRESS

For a job with average working stress, work in publishing or become a farmer or diplomat.

But if you can't stand pressure and want a working life with the top trouser-button loosened, so to speak — get booking. A librarian is reckoned to be the least stressful job — you may even feel relaxed enough to write poetry. It's happened (just Larkin about).

The chart below is rated from 0–10, the higher the number the greater the stress. If you are seeking averageness stay within 4.8–5.2.

Miners rate top of the list because of their hostile environment (below ground that is, surface tension is something else).

Going down the chart, dentists are pretty angst-laden — when they say they can't go on, they often mean it. They have a suicide rate of twice the national average. Apparently too, tax inspectors suffer greater anxiety than the average psychiatric patient. Will we yet see car stickers with S.A.V.E. the P.A.Y.E. man?

Could you come up, please, Miss Robertson, and bring my balls with you?

STRESS CHART

Miner	8.3	Farmer	4.8
Police	7.7	Armed forces	4.7
Construction worker	7.5	Vet	4.5
Journalist	7.5	Civil servant	4.4
Pilot (civil)	7.5	Accountant	4.3
Prison officer	7.5	Engineer	4.3
Advertising	7.3	Estate agent	4.3
Dentist	7.3	Hairdresser	4.3
Actor	7.2	Local government officer	4.3
Politician	7.0	Secretary	4.3
Doctor	6.8	Solicitor	4.3
Taxman	6.8	Artist, designer	4.2
Film producer	6.5	Architect	4.0
Nurse, midwife	6.5	Chiropodist	4.0
Fireman	6.3	Optician	4.0
Musician	6.3	Planner	4.0
Teacher	6.2	Postman	4.0
Personnel	6.0	Statistician	4.0
Social worker	6.0	Lab technician	3.8
Manager (commerce)	5.8	Banker	3.7
Marketing/export	5.8	Computing	3.7
Press officer	5.8	Occupational therapist	3.7
Professional footballer	5.8	Linguist	3.7
Salesman, shop assistant	5.7	Beauty therapist	3.5
Stockbroker	5.5	Vicar	3.5
Bus driver	5.4	Astronomer	3.4
Psychologist	5.2	Nursery nurse	3.3
Publishing	5.0	Museum worker	2.8
Diplomat	4.8	Librarian	2.0

AVERAGE WORKING DAYS LOST

The average number of working days lost through stress alone is one per person per year. Doesn't sound much does it? Until you multiply the figure by the actual working population and it becomes 23 million working days lost a year.

Stress at work can cause high blood pressure and lead to heavy drinking, depression and mental illness or heart disease.

UNIONS

The average person thinks unions in general are out of touch with the views of their members. This is not just the opinion of a few union-bashers but of union and non-union workers alike.

The marked difference between union and non-union opinion comes when discussing a union man's own union. Then 87 per cent of union members think their own union is in touch with its members. It is the others which are adrift. It always is, isn't it?

It's the same with union power. 57 per cent overall and 46 per cent of union members think that unions have too much power. Except when it comes to their own union which is thought to be just about right.

MINING – MOST STRESSFUL JOB

Don't worry luv – he'll be all right.

STRIKES

The average monthly days off due to industrial dispute in 1984 were 2.2 million of which 94 per cent were in coal or related industries.

Apart from mining, the days lost in January 1985 were the lowest monthly total since 1966.

Most people think that the lower number of strikes and the higher percentage of unemployment are not unrelated. 71 per cent think that there are fewer strikes because of fear of unemployment. And only 21 per cent think it's because of improved working relationships between unions and management.

SELF-EMPLOYMENT

An average of 10 per cent of the working population are self-employed, over 2 million people. 25 per cent of these self-employed are women.

2 in 1000 self-employed are West Indian 40 in 1000 are Pakistani/Indian – there are 100 millionaires named Patel!

HOMEWORK

That's not a friend, that's an employer I'm trying out for a few days – Thornton Wilder

This is not self-employment but the number of people, working for other people, working at home.

The average homeworker earns 84p an hour. Many earn only 50p an hour. They'd all be better off working in a factory where the legal minimum hourly rate is £1.70. Home-working computer programmers are top of the executive domestic step ladder with average earnings of £4.63 an hour.

I thought the Government was trying to encourage the self-employed.

UNEMPLOYMENT

Unfortunately it seems the longer you are unemployed, the more likely you are to stay unemployed. New jobs seem to go to the newly out of work.

The average age of an unemployed person is 25; the average length of unemployment is about 28 weeks.

About 1 million men have been unemployed for over a year and 500,000 for over two years. One in three men has a wife who is still working – many of these men now run the home.

The average unemployed person receives only 59 per cent of an employee's income. The longer-term unemployed receive only 39 per cent.

Ten years ago unemployment for blacks and whites was the same, 4 per cent of the working population. Today 13 per cent of white, 25 per cent of black people are out of work.

I'm sorry, Jenkins, but we're going to have to let you lie fallow for a while.

Some achieve redundancy, some have redundancy thrust upon them
but Arthur was *born* redundant.

ACCIDENTS

The average person is safer at work than at home. Most work accidents happen in the manufacturing industry but, relative to working numbers, mining is the most dangerous — 6 times more so than the average work environment. Construction is the next most dangerous industry — it's twice as dangerous as other sectors.

About 400,000 people are involved in work accidents every year. But the good news is that the number is reducing by an average of 10 per cent a year.

LEISURE

But all we ever *do* is go huntin' shootin' and fishin'.

The average person, whether male, female, working, unemployed or retired, has more time for leisure than ever before. It is reckoned that we will spend £50,000 million on leisure in a year. This is an average of £900 for every man, woman and child in the country.

We will soon be spending a quarter of our incomes on leisure (average entrepreneurs – invest in that sports complex quick).

How much time a week do we get to do nothing in? The average working man has about 4 hours a weekday and 11 hours at weekends – a total of 43 hours a week. The average working woman has somewhat less – about 38 hours a week – because she has less time at weekends on account of the cooking, cleaning, washing, etc. that her husband doesn't help her with much (see page 64).

The average housewife is considered to have 51 free hours a week; that's about 7 hours a day during the week.

The unemployed, retired and 'economically inactive' have over 71 hours a week to fill.

The average free time in 1939 (it was called spare time then, reflecting the idea that it was sort of left over from the real business of living which was to work and do chores) was only 30 hours a week. But perhaps one would work longer when one felt the hot breath of war on one's neck.

I wish they wouldn't put this rubbish on so late – I'm dying for an early night.

AN AVERAGE WEEKEND

We do have interests beyond television. Here is a breakdown of a typical weekend at home, with activities listed in order of preference:

	All	Men	Women
1	Watch TV	Watch TV	Watch TV
2	Cook	Read mags	Cook
3	Read Mags	Go for drink	Housework
4	Shop	Shop	Shop
5	Housework	Radio	Read mags
6	Radio	Cook	Radio
7	Go for drink	Visit friends	Read books
8	Visit friends	Read books	Visit friends
9	Read book	Housework	Friends visit
10	Friends visit	Walk/run	Walk/run
11	Walk/run	Records	Knit
12	Records	Friends visit	Go for drink
13	Knit	Car	Records
14	Video	Video	Video
15	Car-care	Garden	Eat out
16	Eat out	DIY	Garden
17	Garden	Eat out	DIY
18	DIY	Watch sport	Dance
19	Play sport	Play sport	Play sport
20	Dance	Dance	Th/cinema

WATCHING THE TELLY

We are one of the great box-watching nations. The average person spends 38 per cent of all leisure time watching TV – a little higher percentage than that in the winter, a little lower in summer.

98 per cent of households have a television – 1 in 6 is black and white only. As a nation we spend an average of more than 20 hours a week watching it – with retired people averaging 7 hours a week more than other groups.

9 in 10 people rate 'watching television' as their main home leisure activity.

UK viewing time is the highest in Europe, but America is way out in front with an average viewing figure of over 31 hours a week per person.

What do we watch on the television? Firstly let's see what we're offered. One-third of all transmission time is taken up by sport, light entertainment and drama. Sport takes up 1 hour in 6, light entertainment 1 in 9 and drama 1 in 18.

1 in 6 would like more sport (1 in 14 less); 1 in 7 would like more light entertainment (1 in 10 less); 1 in 6 would like more drama (on

television this is, but with such viewing figures perhaps in their lives too).

The average viewers split their channel choice thus:

BBC 1   36 per cent 7 hrs 33 mins
BBC 2   13 per cent 2 hrs 44 mins
ITV   45 per cent 9 hrs 21 mins
Channel 4   6 per cent   1 hr 17 mins

A lot of TV is watched in bed. Now 1 in 5 households has a television in the main bedroom.

In the morning a quarter of the population is taking a few minutes of telly with their breakfast at least a few times a week. The 4 —15 year olds are 20 per cent of the morning audience.

Coronation Street averages 20 million viewers a programme — 5 million more than in 1973.

When the ads come on, nearly one-third of viewers switch channels, make themselves a drink, or read. This is particularly true of breaks during light entertainment and sports programmes.

News and current affairs programmes tend not to lose their audiences during the commercials. On average, breaks at the end of programmes lose more viewers than those in mid-programme; men are more likely to stay in front of the set than women.

For the average person the main source of news is television first, daily paper second and radio third.

Finally, to put the box in a global context. There is an average of 3.8 people per television set worldwide – that's 657 million televisions in 162 countries.

Tea!

VIDEO

Currently 1 household in 5 has a video recorder. The average owner uses it solely to record programmes for future viewing. Only 1 in 20 is used primarily for pre-recorded bought tapes.

Video owners do not watch more TV than others, even including items previously recorded. The average length of life of recorded items is 3 days.

RADIO

1 in 2 of the UK population over four years old listens to the radio at one time during the day.

The average person listens to the radio for 9hrs 23 minutes a week, less than half the time spent watching television.

Radio 1, with 31 per cent of listening time, is the most popular station although both BBC and Independent local stations have increased their popularity.

The increase in listening to radio at the time of the Falklands war in 1982 has continued at a slower but steady pace and BBC transmissions, which account for 75 per cent of present listening times, have increased from 24,000 transmission hours to almost 30,000 per annum.

Average position of cinema seats?

CINEMA AND THEATRE

'Nobody goes to the theatre unless he or she has bronchitis.' – James Agate

To be average you will rarely go to the cinema and virtually never to the theatre, not even to see *The Mousetrap*, even though it has been running over thirty years.

About 2 million people go to the cinema or theatre a year – that's only 3½ per cent of the population. The reason generally given (by 5 people in 6) is there is too much drama to be seen in their own living rooms – either on the television live, or through rented videos. However, the blip of extra attendance at the cinema due to the current international success of British films and directors marks this activity as one to watch – for above average growth.

FAVOURITE STAR

That's personality

The average person has a favourite entertainment personality. The most popular media personality is Terry Wogan, who was also voted into third place in a survey to find the Perfect Man, beaten only by Paul Newman and Clint Eastwood.

Women who run him close on the popularity chart are Selina Scott and Felicity Kendal – who has the added appeal (see page 37) of having the most coveted figure.

Entertainment personalities with a lively intelligence will work hard to conceal it. The average Brit does not want more than the iceberg-tip of brainpower to show – that's definitely not entertainment.

Ideally the personality covers it up with an easy charm – but again not too much or he or she becomes labelled smarmy.

READING

Reading isn't an occupation we encourage among police officers. We try to keep paperwork down to a minimum. – Joe Orton

Most people do not read a book at all, ever. The average person would certainly not read this book under normal circumstances – but how many people will be able to resist their own biography!

On any day there are about 11 million people reading a book, 4 million of them library books. Women read more books than men, with romantic novels the most popular, then thrillers, followed by historical and modern novels.

The average man's books are thrillers, then war adventures.

Women buy books for male and female friends, men rarely buy books for others and almost never for a male friend.

The AB's buy more than any other social group – but don't borrow them. Not like the middle classes who borrow madly and are the biggest users of the public libraries.

In a survey of the hundred most borrowed titles, 27 were by Catherine Cookson. Others high in the league included Victoria Holt, Wilbur Smith, Harold Robbins and Jean Plaidy.

Children are the greatest users of libraries – they average 9 books a month compared to 6 a month for adults.

The UK library system is reckoned by many to be the best in the world with about 120 million books for issue. Most adults use it for fiction in a ratio of 3 to 1 with non-fiction.

The average payment to authors under the Public Lending Right scheme was £216. 8000 received this sum – over 5000 authors got less than £100. Only 47 authors received the maximum of £5,000.

But you *must* have a copy of *Apocryphal Tales* – my friend definitely knows someone who saw it on your shelves.

HOME BOOKSHELF

Books on shelves have very much a class relevance and may have little to do with the reading preferences of the owner.

The average home has few owned books. A dictionary, Bible, one or two paperbacks and a one-volume encyclopaedia form the average bookshelf.

In the DE social group, 7 in 100 have none of these books. The upper social groups will probably have all of them.

The average person does not read a book . . .

SPORTS

Anyone for . . . anything?

We are not a great sporting nation. Most of us most of the time don't participate in any sport. Indeed fewer and fewer of us are even watching others play.

PLAYING ABOUT

As opposed to watching others

Walking

In fact our most popular national sporting activity is hardly a sport at all – it's walking. (So as to exclude those who merely walk from the front door to the car or bus stop, walking as a sporting activity is defined by a distance of not less than 2 miles at any one time.)

8 million of us – men slightly more than women – regularly walk this distance purely for exercise and enjoyment. And most of us try to commune a bit with nature at the same time – by walking in a park, by a canal, along leafy roads. It sets us up for an evening round the television.

Swimming

If we group indoor and outdoor swimming together it is the most popular national sport. Nearly 5 million people, split nearly equally between the sexes, swim regularly.

Most swimming is done in indoor public swimming pools. People swimming outdoors prefer the sea and rivers and ponds to outdoor pools, but the risk at these places is high – there are more fatal accidents than with any other sporting activity. Even allowing for its greater popularity it is far more dangerous than soccer, rugby, sailing and horse-riding put together.

Kvick, Doktor — 'ee-a-swallow ee's false teeth.

Snooker and Darts

These two activities are our second most popular sport. They undoubtedly enjoy an increased popularity due to television coverage. Over 3.5 million people, 87 per cent of them men, regularly play snooker and/or billiards. Darts playing is running snooker close with just over 3 million regular players – again a predominantly male occupation.

Sailing and Boating

Sailing and boating together form the third most popular national sport with over 2 million people – with a 3 to 1 ratio of men to women – regularly messing about in boats. But they obviously mess about quite carefully – deaths, at only 3 a year, are the same number as for jogging.

Keep Fit/Yoga

Very few men aspire to be Green (or Greek) Gods. The ratio of women to men who do fit-keeping is the reverse of the snooker figures. Of the 1.3 million who regularly bend, twist and jump up and down to fight the flab, only about 20 per cent are men.

Soccer

This is easily the most popular team sport with 1.2 million men, often in custom-designed strip, pouring on to local pitches every week – at the beginning of every season – wondering, hoping, that this will be the year the team go up for the cup.

Golf/Squash

These sports have in common a national participation level of just over 1 million each and a male predominance of nearly 80 per cent. Golf is *the* most expensive sport in subscription charges, squash the fifth most expensive – this deters no one, both are growth sports.

Other Participation Sports
Other participation sports with a keen and enthusiastic following but by under a million people are:

Sport	average number of participants		
Fishing –	953,000 – mainly men	Athletics – indoor	267,000 – mainly men
Tennis	875,000 – mainly women	Table tennis	647,000 – mainly men
Badminton	875,000 – mainly women	10-pin bowling	438,000 – mainly women
Cycling –	875,000 – mainly women	Horse-riding	394,000 – mainly women
riding a bicycle as opposed to cycling as a serious sport		Bowls	324,000 – mainly men
		Rambling/hiking	324,000 – mainly men
		Cricket	216,000 – mainly men
Athletics – outdoor	857,000 – mainly men	Rugby	210,000 – all men

What luck! I usually just snag a boot.

WATCHING OUT

As opposed to playing about

An average of 1 man in 8 regularly watches a sport — regularly meaning once a month or more often.

Soccer

The most popular sport with almost half the total of all spectators — 18.5 million.

But gates have been falling steadily since the 60s (perhaps because of the mad minority of fans who are off their hinges).

Average gates:

1961–62	11,750 per match
1971–72	10,900 per match
1983–84	7,500 per match
1984–85	7,000 per match

Television has picked up many of the former spectators. Live matches are watched by an average of 8 million people. Recorded matches are watched by an average of 6 million on Saturday, 3 million on Sunday.

I can't imagine what the average spectator looks like

It was his last request, he wanted his ashes thrown at the Manager.

GREYHOUNDS

Going to the dogs

Greyhound racing is the second most popular spectator sport with about 4 million people a year regularly going to the dogs – some 50–60 thousand regular punters.

An average of 24,000 dogs are bred for racing every year with the top dogs commanding prices in excess of £50,000. This is big business because the betting is big business – an estimated £200 million a year is staked on dog racing.

MOTOR SPORT
Vroom for expansion

Motor-car and motor-cycle sports are growing in popularity as spectator sports and now rival horseriding with about 4 million spectators a year.

HORSERACING
Falling off horses

The average number of spectators at race meetings has declined slowly to its current level of just under 4 million people a year. But it is still the third most popular spectator sport.

The average punter, however, is increasing his (3 in 4 are men) off-course betting throughout the 11,000-odd betting shops. The average spend is very high relative to other gambling pursuits – in excess of £21 a week which, when put against the £3.15 a week spent by 1 in 3 gamblers, indicates the high level of investment at the top end of the market.

Most gamblers admit they've lost more than they've won, whatever method they choose. 42 per cent go by the form book which still leaves the average punter to make his choice with a favourite name, or jockey or lucky pin.

On Derby day for instance, 14 million people will be hoping they've picked the winner; 8 million at the bookies, 6 million in the office and pub sweepstakes. The average bet will be nearly £3 per man; 77p per woman.

OTHER SPECTATOR SPORTS

What will be the average sport to watch in a year or so?

Rugby League attendances are growing – up to 40 per cent – but the sport still hasn't breached the wall south – where Union rules.

Rugby Union attendances are up too – a more modest 7 per cent.

The indoor events up-and-comer has to be basketball, with a 27-fold increase in spectator numbers.

Snooker events are often full to capacity but numbers are necessarily small because halls are usually small. 11 million watch peak matches on the television.

CRICKET

Test/County matches

Attendances are greatly influenced by the weather and although good in 1984 (about 1 million) in 1982 they were down to 780,000.

BINGO

Ahhhh!

This is the second most popular form of gambling, although it's declined from its high of 5.5 million to 3.8 million. 1 in 8 women are regularly 'eyes down' and hoping to win the jackpot with their average spend of £2.

The industry is about the same size as the football pools market, turning over about £450 million through some 1500 clubs.

FOOTBALL POOLS

Looking for a lucky dip

This is the most popular form of gambling in the UK. 8 million people indulge in it regularly – happily filling in their coupons crossly in the hope of landing the £1,000,000 jackpot.

The average stake is just £1.13 a week. That's a turnover of about £500 million a year.

GARDENING

Forlawn figure

The average gardener hates gardening. We spend over £500 million a year on our gardens and gardening equipment and yet 2 out of 3 of us consider gardening 'outdoor housework'. Women are as likely to do all the gardening – including mowing the grass – as men.

But who said men were ungentlemanly? The average man would certainly not buy his wife a manual mower – 9 in 10 mowers now purchased are electrically or mechanically powered.

DIY

Mrs Fixit is here

The average DIY job is as likely to be done by a woman as a man. The average unisex repair job is re-soling of shoes. 60 per cent of all households do this – an even higher percentage in the under-24 age group where 7 in 10 do it.

DIY repairs, as opposed to making or 'improving' things, are more commonly undertaken by AB and C_1 groups than C_2 and DE groups.

The Scots are the least likely to undertake common DIY repairs such as children's toys, books, satchels etc; the Welsh the most likely.

The average DIY-er often has more enthusiasm than skill: take electrical repairs – 200 fires are caused annually by wrongly wired-up plugs. The wire colour scheme is often misunderstood. Or repairing plumbing – 55,000 houses are flooded every year. Or home decorating – 15,000 people fall off ladders every year. Or car maintenance – the car jack seems to be more nimble and quick than its owner – it collapses on 1000 legs a year.

AVERAGE HOLIDAY

The average holiday is spent in the UK.

On average when we go away on holiday we stay here. 3 in 4 holidays are taken in the UK, with England taking 60 per cent of UK holiday makers.

40 per cent of households don't leave home at all, which hasn't changed since 1970, and about the same proportion have never been abroad. This is odd in that most other leisure activities have grown greatly in the last two decades and here are over 20 million people homebound. The reason is cost.

Oh, we probably had a terrible time, but when you're on holiday who cares?

The average holiday takes up 20 per cent of all leisure expenditure with an average cost per adult of £330. This includes hotel, travel, food, everything. For the average person there is really only one month to go on holiday: August. In this month in the UK 11 million people are on holiday.

Hi Dee Hi

One in 25 who goes anywhere, goes to a holiday camp in the UK — one in 100 goes to a holiday camp in Europe.

In January and February foreign holidays exceed UK ones.

It seems holidays are habit forming. Once you start taking them it is difficult to stop. Of the group who do take holidays, 25 per cent take 2 holidays and about 10 per cent 3 holidays a year.

Holidays are very much a class issue with AB's averaging 33 days away, C_1's 20 days, C_2's 16 days and DE's 15 days.

AVERAGE HOLIDAY ABROAD

9 in 10 of all holidays abroad are spent in Europe, with 4 in 10 going to Spain. The second most popular place is France, with Greece rating third. As a holiday agent put it drily 'Our customers go mostly to Spain — for

It gets more crowded every year — but there's still something rather attractive about the place.

an upset tummy; or France – to be ignored or insulted; or thirdly to Greece – to get sunstroke.'

50 per cent of the holidays are a total package costing £200. Spending money is on top of this.

Children are much more certain about where they want to holiday – 92 per cent want to go abroad and to America in particular. They don't go, though, mostly they holiday in the UK – as you'd expect, that's where their parents are.

The UK as a holiday choice by children gets only 8 per cent of the votes, as do Australia and New Zealand.

with thanks and acknowledgements to the *Daily Mail*

Only twenty yards from the beach, the brochure said. Lovely sea views . . .

Nice to get away, isn't it?

On these trips abroad Henry's always been prone to tummy bugs . . .

SKIING HOLIDAYS

Off piste

Actors say 'break a leg' to each other at the start of a play because it is unlucky to say 'good luck'. Holiday makers may well say 'good luck' to each other at the start of their skiing holiday. But it doesn't do any good. An average of 1 in 25 holiday skiers breaks a leg. It is not known whether most of them are plastered before as well as after the accident.

We went for the full two weeks.

HOLIDAY LUGGAGE

Travelling heavy

Women pack it in far too readily – when going on holiday. The average woman will often wear only 25 per cent of the clothes she has taken. Anxious mothers are the biggest packers but children often have a suitable case for treatment by squeezing in too many play items.

SSEEX

MAKING LOVE – FIRST TIME

The average girl believes herself to be in love with a wonderful guy and makes love the first time to a steady boyfriend. But 25 per cent get carried away by the moment.

Another 22 per cent feel themselves pressured into it by the boyfriends – a case, it seems, of she who hesitates is won. Afterwards there is the worry – 50 per cent of girls have no protection the first time.

Although 80 per cent of couples subsequently take precautions, this still leaves over 100,000 girls regularly risking pregnancy – often with blind faith in their boyfriends who say 'it'll be all right!'

There must be a way of making it illegal for girls to reach puberty without their parents' consent.

FIRST TIME ENJOYMENT

Sex, the first time, is not a satisfactory experience for the average couple. The cinema has let us down, life does not go into soft focus. One feels none of the imagery of erupting volcanoes, crashing waterfalls or even koala bears frolicking. The more accurate analogy seems to be the dodg'em car ride at a busy funfair; an unexpected bump here, swerving and missing there and the whole thing over much sooner than expected.

The younger the couple the less likely they are to enjoy the first time. Rough justice, you may consider, when so many of them legally shouldn't be doing it anyway. Over 25, the few of either sex without previous experience think 'it's better than expected'.

But here's to the 10 per cent who enjoy it a great deal the first time.

Men and boys are particularly reticent on this first time question – lots of blanks on questionnaires – leaving the distinct impression that they do not feel they acquitted themselves very well, satisfying neither themselves nor their partners.

ENGAGEMENT

The average suitor still proposes formally – over a meal usually and sometimes doing the one-knee trick.

The average length of engagement is 19 months. This is not as significant as it used to be. In the 1950s engagement may have allowed a little more freedom but certainly was not a licence for full sexual relations.

It isn't now, but for a different reason. Consummation has already taken place in 98 per cent of cases. About 1 in 4 couples will already be living together by the time they marry, probably for about a year.

WEDDING CLOTHES

The average bride insists on a wedding dress – even when getting married in a register office. And it has to be new; only 3 brides in 100 will accept hired clothes.

For him a lounge suit is the average attire. Only 3 in 10 wear morning dress but the use is growing. In Scotland 1 groom in 4 wears a kilt.

WEDDING CEREMONY

I have always thought that every woman should marry, but no man. – Benjamin Disraeli

The average wedding now is not in a church, it's in a register office. 52 per cent get married here – and the percentage is growing because of the number of divorcees remarrying. If, however, it is the first time for both of you and you want to be truly average, you must still get married in church.

Only 1 in 3, though, get married in church for 'religious reasons'. Just as many do it for the pageantry, the spectacle – which must bring a warm glow to the sentimental heart of the wedding photographer who is going to charge over £100 to capture the happy moment on film.

AVERAGE AGE OF BRIDE AND GROOM

The average age to get married is at 22.3 years for the bride and 24.5 years for the groom. Shocked as Romeo and Juliet would have been at the thought of another decade of restraint there is worse news. The average age is rising steadily. Twenty years ago girls were in their 21st year on average when they wed.

But Romeo's picture of self-control would not be accurate. The reason people are marrying later is that they are co-habiting sooner and longer before marriage.

And which one of you is the bride?

WEDDING GUESTS

. . . Guests must be chosen as carefully as the wine. – Saki

You should be a wedding guest, if you really aim to be average, once every 18 months. Check your diary. And at your next wedding try to do a quick head count to see that you are mixing with the right quantity: the average number of guests at a wedding is 105.

COST OF WEDDING

Throwing confetti like money

The chart below tells all. The average cost of the average wedding is now over £2,500.

The Scots, as with several other averages throughout this book, seem to go against their popular characteristic by having the most lavish weddings with an average of 160 guests.

The cost of each guest's present is on average £34.50.

THE WEDDING

Average Costs

Item	Ave. Cost £	Traditional Payer
Engagement ring	232	Groom
Engagement announcement	39	Bride's father
Stag party	62	Groom
Hen party	40	Bride
Invitations	53	Bride's father
Bride's dress etc	232	Bride's father
Trousseau	182	Bride's father
Bride's mother's clothes	127	Bride's father
Bridesmaids' clothes	144	Bride's father
Groom's clothes	89	Groom
Wedding rings	74	Bride/Groom
Flowers	77	Bride's father
Cars	87	Bride's father
Fees, licences	23	Groom
Press announcement	48	Bride's father
Photographs	128	Bride's father
Video	114	Bride's father
Presents ushers/b'maids	84	Groom
Reception hire	50	Bride's father
Food	514	Bride's father
Drink	197	Bride's father
Cake	61	Bride's father
WEDDING TOTAL	2,763	
Honeymoon	256	Bride/Groom
Equipping home		
a) Presents	3,520	Guests
b) Other	922	Bride/Groom
Deposit on house/flat	2,500	Bride/Groom

On average the bride's father does not pay all the reception costs. They are shared by both families. Both families too contribute to the bride and groom's costs, especially the honeymoon.

AVERAGE HONEYMOON

Newly-weds on average allow just 9 days in which to get to know each other as Mr and Mrs. In the Biblical sense of course they've known each other for some time.

As they drive from the reception, perhaps with a kipper tied to the exhaust pipe and a boot bouncing behind, they head for a UK hotel – not many combine the exotic with the erotic.

If they do venture abroad the place which is hot favourite is Majorca, with the Channel Isles second choice and Paris third.

APRÈS HONEYMOON

Still over the moon, honey?

The average newly-married couple come back to their own home. They have already saved £2½ thousand with a building society and taken out a mortgage on Chez Nous Mark I. 2 couples in 10 return to shared accommodation – usually with parents; 1 couple in 10 return to a purchased flat.

I have a feeling this survey was done during the summer.

FREQUENCY OF SEX

Married couples should make love 104 times a year. – Martin Luther

In fact our national average is once every 3.8 days – 96 times annually. Now this isn't to say that many don't do it a lot more times than this.

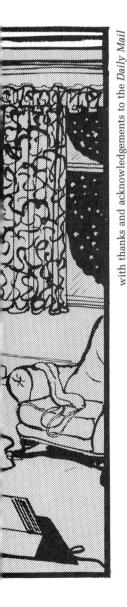

with thanks and acknowledgements to the *Daily Mail*

INTERCOURSE AVERAGES

Age	Frequency – every . . .	No. times a year
16–24	2.5 days	146
25–34	3.2 days	115
35–44	3.6 days	102
45–54	4.4 days	83
55+	5.2 days	70

If you relate the above figures to the total UK population it means that every day the country reverberates to the rhythms of 2,965,970 couples making love. Can we be really sure that it's the waves which lap the land and not the other way around?

But statistics and surveys can be a little disturbing here. In some surveys it seems that men have sex more often than their partners!

On average, it seems, the older you get the less you want, and the converse of that, is the general rule. Teenagers, in the same way that children with a new toy play with it all the time, tend to make love much more often than the average.

Luther hates Superman

In fact over 500,000 couples – 125,000 of them aged 55+ – make love daily; a situation Martin Luther would have considered devil-inspired. And he would have been bitterly disappointed in the Scots whose coupling rate is conspicuously higher at all age levels.

A big change in sexual attitudes is that of women who now admit the importance of sex to them. 33 per cent claim it is important, very important. 20 per cent say that they get frustrated without sex at least once a week.

Women in the south and south-east seem to like sex more often – and average up to 4 times a week.

London women seem to have the highest love-making rate of all – with 28 per cent reckoning to indulge 5 or more times a week. They contrast with Midlands women where about the same percentage have sex once a week or less.

A total of 970,000 couples, 1 couple in 14, never have sex together; about the same number have it once a month or less.

DISUNITED STATES OF AMERICA

Close encounters only

The average woman in America prefers a cuddle to full sexual relations.

It seems that men are too much the takers and that 'How was it for you?' – standard phraseology in most American movies – is only standard phraseology in most American movies. In truth, the men, it seems, don't care. Women yearn for more foreplay . . . a little romance. As the other cliché has it – 'shouldn't we talk about this?'

TIME OF LOVE MAKING

'Up to half an hour' is the nearest we can get to the average time taken for making love.

44 per cent of couples put their sex life into this rather loosely defined time-span – 3 seconds, 3 minutes and 30 minutes all come within this definition, which offers scope enough for a variety of techniques.

A further 30 per cent take a more leisurely 'hour or so' and a further 3 per cent claim to prolong the activity for 'hours on end'.

Perhaps the reason for the general vagueness about time is that the average couple are not clockwatching.

Two minutes is the average time for humans between what is medically called intromission and ejaculation.

Orang-utans average ten minutes, which often causes conflicts and jealousies between the males. Chimpanzees on the other hand average seven seconds and the males live harmoniously together.

The opinion of the female apes is not known.

ENERGY USED

The average person may well expend up to 200 calories when making love – a game of squash burns up 400 calories. And if you are one of that less than 5 per cent who like unusual places, and make love on the squash court, well . . .

BEST PHYSICAL TIMES

8 am — Male sex hormones reach peak production
2–4 pm — top physical performance potential
1–7 pm — mental power at optimum level
8 pm — maximum resistance to disease

So, to get the best from your average condition, set the alarm for 7.30 am if you want to procreate (this allows half-an-hour for foreplay). In the Australian outback the alarm can be set for 7.59 am, foreplay there, it is said, being reduced to, 'You awake, Sheila?'

Early afternoon – try to get back in the sack if you really want the earth to move, this is the time you are really flying. Also you will be approaching your cerebral peak too, so sensibly you will leap out of bed afterwards to impress clients, customers, patients, etc.

And if you are going home to a husband, wife, child or mother with a cold, make sure you arrive home late – when your immunity is at its highest.

Yoo hoo, Beryl! It's your 3 o'clock earthmover.

AVERAGE PLACE OF MAKING LOVE

That place is bed for a massive 96 per cent. If this seems too tediously dull, other very average places are: the living room, 78 per cent; elsewhere in the house, 46 per cent; in the car, 41 per cent; and al fresco, 31 per cent.

Obviously for unmarrieds not co-habiting, there is often the problem of opportunity and hence the statistic of 1 per cent of unfortunate unmarrieds – unmarried to each other, that is – who have to fit it in at work, presumably in the time between old workaholic Watson, or whoever, leaving his office and the cleaners arriving.

WHEN

At night, almost invariably. 60 per cent may make love first thing in the morning.

119

But the *really* great thing is the shower afterwards.

THE IMPORTANCE OF SEX

80 per cent think sex fulfilment is important. 40 per cent think it possible still to have a good marriage without a good, active sex life. 40 per cent think the media make them feel inadequate. This means millions feel inadequate but in fact are perfectly normal.

Most women consider love/affection in the general sense as the most important element of their sex life – particularly in the 45–54 age group. They like to take the sexual initiative sometimes although 8 per cent of husbands usually refuse their wives when they do.

Well, at least it was a personal best.

FANTASTIC LOVEMAKING

It may give many a husband pause for thought that his wife may be away with the fairies at the very moment he is thinking they are at their closest.

The average wife fantasises during lovemaking. The fantasies usually concern an ideal love in an ideal environment. It may well be with her husband or another man she knows or even a famous person.

Very few fantasies involve violence or forced submissions but quite a high percentage – 1 in 14 – involves being watched or having sex with several men at once. Rarely are the fantasies concerned with ethnic changes in their partner, or with a complete stranger or with another woman.

A midfield dynamo shouldn't have *that* many nagging groin strains.

AVERAGE CHANGE WANTED

Many men and women would like more sex, which is ruination for one of the original cornerstones of men's jokes – the 'tell him you've got a headache' variety. The truth is that 1 in 3 wives would like sex more often. Generally they think their friends enjoy greater sexual activity – they would like a slice of the action too. As the less-than-satisfied wife put it, 'I've two weeks to live – my husband's away on business.'

The reason for a husband's disappointing performance is that *he* is too tired. 3 in 10 husbands are – often.

Against this is the 2 out of every 3 couples who agree that quality is better than quantity.

1 in every 5 would like his/her partner to be more enthusiastic.

AFFAIRS

Wouldn't it be lover-ly?

No matter how happily married a woman may be, it often pleases her to discover a nice man who wishes she were not – as H L Mencken put it.

An average of 3 in 10 wives would agree with that – having taken at least one lover since they married. Half this number have had two or more affairs.

Statistically then, 1½ wives in 10 are having an affair at this moment – just what does half a mistress get up to?

And just as to the great lemming question – why do they do it? – the answer is unsatisfactory. Most of the wives with lovers – 60 per cent of them – claim they have an affair for the excitement; but the same percentage claim it is not as sexually satisfying as their marriage is.

Husbands on average have somewhat more of the wanderlust in them. 2 in 10 are likely to be having an affair at this moment (which, while we cannot condone it, does do away with those untidy halves).

Frankly, if we'd known Gerald was gay, we wouldn't have come to his wife-swapping party.

HOMOSEXUALS

The average ratio of homosexual to heterosexual is 1 in 8.

This proportion is accepted by most gay groups who further maintain that lesbians are 1 in 8 of this figure, that is, 1 in 64 in relation to heterosexuals.

The homosexual population is thus about 2.6 million; lesbians number about 330,000.

127

AVERAGE AGE: 200

A scientist reckons that in time we will be able to control the ageing process to enable us to achieve an average age of 200 years.

But a pre-requisite of that would be no sex until aged 80.

with thanks and acknowledgements to the *Daily Mail*

I've waited till I'm eighty and you have a headache?

SOCIAL

TRUST

I don't believe it

With everybody, it seems, grinding away with one axe or another, who is it we can turn to to tell us the truth? The average person is far more likely to believe 'an ordinary man or woman in the street' (i.e. an average person) than one of the professional persuaders such as journalists, business leaders, politicians and trades union leaders.

About 3 in 4 people say you cannot believe what these people say.

Although we are a pretty irreligious lot as a nation we still seem to believe that God is Truth; at least his full-time executives are. The average person believes a clergyman. 85 per cent of us think clergymen don't lie.

Doctors, teachers and judges are the next most believed-in beings.

Now do you see why I like slim, humorous and kind men?

DESIRABLE QUALITIES IN A MAN

These are the qualities the average woman considers to be important in a man:

	Percentage of younger women	Percentage of older women
Kindness	85	88
Humour	80	84
Faithfulness	77	70
IQ	51	59
Education	19	30
Sexual prowess	19	16
Money	12	20
Strength	10	11
Good looks	7	2
Dominance	4	4

The chart shows that women stay remarkably consistent to their early values as they get older. They change their opinions about sex and money, but not much.

In addition to being kind and humorous, the ideal man would be slim. Small hips and bottom are a definite preference, particularly among the younger women. Only 16 per cent of older women consider them — probably because they are faced with a fat accompli!

THE UNFEELING BRITISH

Out of touch

The average UK adult is not a toucher. In a restaurant survey in one hour:

A British couple from London did not touch each other at all

An American couple from Jacksonville touched 8 times

A Puerto Rican couple from San Juan touched 20 times

A couple from Paris, France touched 110 times

So, natives of Britain, let's take it again from the top – once more with feeling.

WORDS

What d'you call it

The average person has a working vocabulary of about 4,000 words – less than 1/100th of the number contained in the *Oxford Dictionary*.

George Bernard Shaw was thought to have had at his command some 50,000 words.

NUMBERS

Sum problem

An average of 1 adult in 3 cannot divide 5 into 65 in his or her head. Nor add 1 to 6,399.

BREAKFAST CEREAL

Oat Culture

Sam Johnson, who defined oats as a grain which in England is generally given to horses but in Scotland supports the people, would be shocked at the modern breakfast.

The average household now buys bran (oat) cereal at least once a month — it is one of the fastest-growing product lines of the British food industry.

TEA

... We drink too much tea. I see in this the slow revenge of the Orient, which has diverted the Yellow River down our throats. — J B Priestley

Although tea consumption is declining, 6 out of 10 hot drinks are the traditional cuppa — made with tea bags in most cases.

If you think of the shape of Great Britain as roughly that of a dumped wet tea bag, you'll remember the further north you go the less they use leaf (packet) tea. 78 per cent of all cups of tea are made with tea bags in Scotland; 70 per cent in the north and 64 per cent in the south.

COFFEE

Coffee is the fastest growing non-alcoholic beverage, with the average person drinking 2–3 cups a day.

Ground coffee has doubled in sales and instant coffee use increased by 17 per cent over the last 5 years.

132

AVERAGE TEA TIME

. . . And is there honey still for tea?

Tea-time has gone. For the average Brit, the traditional tea of bread and butter, jam and honey, cakes and pastries is in its terminal stages.

It is now the least most important meal of the day compared to its top 3 position – behind breakfast and lunch – only 5 years ago.

Perhaps a new word for a new meal-time is required. About a quarter of tea-times now include a meat or fish dish, fresh fruit and usually dessert. This is primarily due to children having their main meal earlier with adults eating later. Also, in families with unemployed heads-of-household, meals tend to be eaten earlier.

AVERAGE ALCOHOLIC DRINK

The average man drinks 5 glasses of wine a week, 4½ pints of beer and one nip of the hard stuff. The average woman drinks 3 glasses of wine, half a pint of beer and a single spirit every 2 weeks. This is where your modest claim to be an average drinker may be put to the test!

We used to have a healthy wine consumption in days of yore. In about 1370 when John of Gaunt was too busy defending Aquitaine and Bordeaux from the French even to consider how many pubs were going to be named after him, the UK population, then about 4 million, drank copious quantities of claret.

Nowadays our consumption can't bear comparison with France's, although the news from there is that only 44.5 per cent of men now drink wine regularly with their meals; about 50 per cent now turn to water. Wine consumption has slumped from 140 litres a year to less than 100 litres per person – eau yes!

EATING OUT

What does the average couple eat on the big night out – which on average is once a month?

They start with prawn cocktail or avocado, followed by 'something traditional' such as roast beef and two veg or steak, chips and beans. It's rounded off with ice-cream or Black Forest gateau and the whole lot washed down by a bottle of white wine. The bill will be between £6.50 and £7.00 a head.

If they fancy something exotic, Chinese food is the most popular followed by Indian, then Italian.

He can be pretty mean when he takes his wife out to dine . . .

They know me here, so whatever you do, don't let on that you're my wife.

Your usual table, sir.

AVERAGE BATHS

The average man baths about 3 times a week, woman about 4.

We can dismiss the idea of bathing just for cleanliness. The average Brit likes a soak — long enough for finger ends and toes to get that sultana-skin crinkle. Men average 26 minutes a bath; women 24 minutes.

It's taken me a long time to persuade Harry of the importance of hygiene but he now visits a sauna twice weekly.

This means an average person, living an average-length life will spend over a year in the bath.

Half the population never showers. Northerners shower much more than Midlanders and Southerners. Students are the cleanest sector of society – they take the longest baths and shower more often.

Britain is the cleanest nation in Europe and possibly the world. Certainly as a nation we use more soap than any other European country, an average of 7 bars a year per household.

The French are lowest on the scale. Apart from having 10 per cent of households which don't buy any soap at all, 2 out of 5 Frenchmen don't possess a toothbrush – a fact in itself to make the average Englishman bristle.

41 per cent of British men use a deodorant compared to a national low in West Germany where only 18 per cent use an anti-perspirant regularly and a high in Canada where 85 per cent of all men use one regularly.

The next time you land in a cow pat, do it on a Friday, that's our normal bath night.

IN THE LAVATORY

Loo'd behaviour

We each flush the lavatory 4 or 5 times a day. We didn't, as market research questionnaires put it, 'probe' when given this information.

We suggest interested persons conduct further research at their own convenience.

We can say that flushing the lavatory costs the average household over 5p a flush.

TOILET PAPER

France is a country where the money falls apart in your hands and you can't tear the toilet paper. – Billy Wilder

So much for the French. The British nation on the other hand has definitely gone soft. A mere ten years ago 50 per cent of our toilet paper was of the hard, shiny type – and in offices and factories it was 90 per cent.

Today 87 per cent of all toilet paper is of the soft tissue variety. On average we use two-thirds of a roll a week.

Have you got one in Chelsea colours?

CIGARETTES

So much puffery

The average number of cigarettes smoked today in the UK is just over 14 per smoker per day. The number is steadily declining. In 1978 it was 16 a day, in 1968 it was 20.

At the moment about a third of the adult population smokes – a greater percentage of adult men than women but more young girls than boys are taking up the habit.

20 per cent aged between 11 and 18 say they smoke, against 14 per cent of boys. Two-thirds of young people said they had never smoked; most of the smokers said they would like to stop.

Only 6–7 per cent of young people were diehard smokers who had no intention of trying to give up.

On average after a national No Smoking day about 10 per cent of those who give up are still not smoking more than two months afterwards.

I said . . . do you mind if I smoke?

While we are here in the average bedroom, let's look around. There is not much room to move about: the average measurements are 12ft by 9ft.

There are usually three items of luggage stored – either under the bed or on top of the wardrobe.

CLOTHES
AVERAGE WARDROBE

For women:	10 dresses
	6 skirts
	12 blouses/shirts
	7 sweaters
	2 coats
	3 pairs slacks
	7 pairs shoes
For men:	3 suits
	2 jackets
	11 shirts
	5 sweaters
	5 pairs trousers
	1 coat
	4 pairs shoes

Many husbands reading the above will feel reassured that their complaints about the size of their wives' wardrobes were justified – but they had better check first that they only have one coat or four pairs of shoes . . .

AVERAGE BED WEAR

On the bed is the average couple's nightwear. Identical nightshirts. They must be under 35. Over 35s are still into pyjamas. Growing in popularity amongst the under 35s are boxer shorts and T-shirts. Again unisex cut.

The average couple now possess at least one garment which doubles for lounging and nightwear.

Twenty years ago the average woman possessed one heavy housecoat/dressing gown. It's still popular with fifty-year-olds and over but only rarely with younger women – probably the spread of central heating has something to do with it.

AVERAGE UNDERWEAR
Underwear, underworn

Although there's a move by women towards unisex vest and pants, the average woman still buys, on average, 9 pairs of panties a year.

Bra sales have fallen by 6 million since 1970 although the population aged 12 plus has increased by more than half a million in this time.

CASUAL CLOTHES

Haven't you anything a little *less* casual?

Striding Out

When they first offered their cheap, rough trouser material to the world, the merchants de Nîmes little knew the clothing revolution they were starting.

The most popular item of casual wear in the UK is a pair of jeans. An average of 2 in 5 men and 2 in 5 women have bought jeans within the last year. 75 per cent of all people under 25 have at least 2 pairs of jeans in current use.

Above the jeans, if you are an average male, you will wear a casual shirt (which has a 20 per cent chance of coming from M&S). 1 man in 5 will wear a T-shirt, 3 girls in 5 will.

AVERAGE PET

Cats and dogs reigning

The average household hasn't got one.

Anybody who hates dogs and kids can't be all bad, W C Fields said, and most of us think he was at least half right – 52 per cent of all households have no pet at all.

In the 48 per cent of households which are petted, the most popular is a dog. Nearly 6 million of them share their well known companionship with us and spread their well known daily do's throughout the country – amounting to an incredible 1000 tons a day.

Dog licences cost 37½p but about £1.50 to collect and administer. The difference is made up from the general rates, which makes non-dog owners very angry, especially if they've just trodden . . .

AVERAGE DOG

Labradors are the most popular, followed by spaniels, followed by German Shepherds (Alsatians, the former name, is on the way out because everybody knows a German product is good quality), followed by collies.

Posh dogs are in. The Bitser's days are numbered. 60 per cent of UK dogs have a pedigree – which may well put them in a higher social category than their owners.

The average dog owner spends over £1 a week on dog food. The canned pet food market is as big as that for sliced bread or eggs. On average about 4,000 complaints are made about barking dogs every week and yet a dog's hearing is 3 times more sensitive than a human's – a cat's is 5 times.

A Nip in the Air
Not Japanese parachutists but the number of people bitten by dogs every day. It is over 500 – and these are hospital cases only, the real number is probably double.

Dogs Bow Wowt
In one of their less inscrutable policies the Chinese have decided how to solve their dog problems – they have abolished them. Owners have had to present their dogs to an official receiver.

They Rue the Day
In Paris it costs ratepayers £2 million a year to have the streets cleared of excrement left by the capital's 600,000 dogs. It must be extra galling that 1 dog in 4 in France is a British breed.

141

CATS

Cats are the second most popular pet with a total of 5½ million in 1 in 5 households. And those households tend to be in the upper social group. Dogs as pets are more popular with C_2, DE households.

We use the phrase a dog's life to describe hardship and deprivation. It's a wonder we don't have cat's life to describe the opposite. UK cats lead the most cosseted lives. They are flapped, littered and fed to the purr of £380 million a year. The biggest selling grocery item in the UK is a cat food and cats may well smile enigmatically at our phrase cat-nap. On average a cat sleeps 14 hours a day.

Yes, I like a cat – doesn't everyone.

BUDGERIGARS

An average of 1 household in 14 has a budgerigar. This means that although there are over 2 million of them in the UK, you as an average person should not have one at all (and never call them budgies says bird expert, Geoff Capes, with the convincing argument of being Britain's international shot putter and strongest man). 8 in 10 budgerigars live in households of 1 or 2 people who are council tenants, elderly, living in a flat or terraced house. But the birds still have £10 million a year spent on them.

FISH AND OTHERS

As with budgerigars, an average of 1 household in 14 has a fish. But although in Walt Disney's memorable phrase, there's a natural hootchy kootchy to a goldfish, they do have a 'lifespan problem'. It's very short – as is the duration of the interest span of the average young owner.

Rabbits, hamsters, gerbils, guinea pigs and mice do not feature on the Average Pet scale at all and generally ownership of them is declining. But one sector of the market is growing. Read on for the latest in pet development . . .

You must have done *something* to upset him!

Sit!

REPTILE PETS

Things are creeping up on us

Reptiles will soon be average pets, is the claim of experts who see them equalling the tropical fish market. Most popular are: the fire bellied toad from China; the geeko, a tree lizard from Madagascar; and the giant stick insect from New Guinea.

The average buyers are couples without children who want 'background movement'. South American anacondas cost £200 and can grow to 30ft in length – maybe they can double as draught excluders?

AVERAGE CAR

Mean motoring

If you own a Ford Escort saloon, your claim to the average person title will be much enhanced. It was the best-selling car in Britain in 1984 and they are still selling well.

As one Ford-awed dealer put it – 'We move more Escorts than all the computer dating agencies put together.'

Almost every car maker is claiming it is producing the 'car of the people'. Hitler of course did the same and VW Beetles were produced in the same shape for thirty years. He, though, tried to manufacture people to fit the cars.

Time was in the UK when the Cortina dominated the car sales charts – with more than 30 per cent of the market. John Betjeman knew it well:

> I am a young executive no cuffs than mine
> are cleaner
> I own a slimline briefcase and drive the
> firm's Cortina

Now no model achieves even 10 per cent of the total market. Of the 16 million cars on the roads, 11 million are UK made – and 6 million are reckoned to be worth under £1,000.

Asked what car he would prefer to be driving, the average driver chooses a Porsche or a Jaguar.

There's nothing basically wrong – it's just spoilt.

AVERAGE MOTORING

Top sellers
1 Ford Escort
2 Vauxhall Cavalier
3 Ford Fiesta
4 Austin/MG Metro
5 Ford Sierra
6 Austin/MG Maestro
7 Vauxhall Astra
8 Vauxhall Nova
9 Ford Orion
10 Volvo 300 series
11 Austin/MG Montego
12 VW Polo
Sales in 84: 1,749,650
About 60 per cent imported

Most households have a car. The national average is 60 per cent of all households but north and south figures are quite different. Fewer than 50 per cent of northern families have a car; over 75 per cent of southern families do.

Sympathise with the manufacturer who tries to find a name which everybody will like for his new model. Nova sounds fine doesn't it – except that in Latin America, where they tried to sell it, it means 'it won't go'.

RUNNING COSTS

It's enough to give you internal combustion. The cost of running the average car is 24p a mile. If it's an un-average two-litre car you run, the cost is 33p per mile.

DRIVING LIMIT
O.T.T.

The average man reaches the legal driving limit at 5 units of alcohol; the average woman at 3 units – assuming an average reaction to drink.

Half a pint of beer, a small sherry or martini, a single spirit or a glass of wine are each equivalent to one unit of alcohol. On average both men and women over-estimate their capacity by 20 per cent.

BREATHALYSER TEST

The average motorist who is breathalysed is not over the limit. About 30 per cent are – although more than 50 per cent have had a drink.

DRIVING TEST
L of a time

You have a 50–50 chance of passing your driving test first time as an average person. You can improve your chances by going west – the pass percentage is highest in the Bristol area. It is lowest in London and Yorkshire.

About 1 in 3 adults can drive.

AVERAGE TRAVEL

Most of us agree with Mr Toad: 'The real way to travel! The only way to travel . . . O bliss! O my, O my. . . '.

Yes, the average person travels by motor car.

In 1953 the car accounted for about 30 per cent of getting from A to B. Its use has grown every decade and now 83 per cent of all motorised travel is done by car. Even the 40 per cent of British households who don't own a car contrive to travel by it as passengers – eschewing public transport.

But although 6 in 10 households own a car only 25 per cent of adults have the use of it whenever they want. After all, as Robert Bradbury put it, what is a pedestrian but a man with two cars – one being driven by his wife, the other by one of the children.

And we are a great nation of walkers. 4 in every 10 journeys are on foot. Less than 1 in 10 is by local bus and only 1 in 100 is by train. Buses and trains have about the same percentage of travellers now, between 7 and 8 per cent, as the bicycle had 30 years ago. Bicycles now have just 1 per cent of the movement market.

The average household spends £23 a week on travel. This sum includes £11 to run a vehicle, another £8 to purchase it; bus/coach fares of £1, and rail fare £1.

The average distance travelled per journey is 6 miles and about 50 per cent of all journeys are on leisure or sports pursuits.

I'll say this for Fred Higgins — he's got exquisite manners . . .

ROAD ACCIDENTS

On average over 6,000 people are killed in accidents every year — 81,000 are seriously injured; 248,000 are slightly injured.

The average accident occurs at 25 mph in a built-up area in daylight, at a junction. Hitting a stationary object at this speed is like falling from 20ft high on to a hard surface.

Road casualties per minute over a 24-hour period average 234; between 4 and 5pm they average 438.

Two-wheeled vehicles average 1 in 12 of all road accidents. Many drivers are unsure of their vehicle's performance. For example, to enter a traffic stream going at 30 mph a moped

needs a clear space of 100 yards to avoid impeding the traffic flow. In a survey, police asked moped drivers what they thought the space had to be: the highest said 40 yards; the average was 27 yards.

Average cost of accidents:
Per fatality: £127,000
Per serious injury: £9,000
Slight injury: £4,500

These figures added up for the nation as a whole represent 2 per cent of public expenditure, i.e. £2,631 million. This costs the average household £128 a year.

146

Don't worry, I don't think I'm seriously hurt!

No wonder they have so many accidents — can't keep to their own side of the road.

MUGGING

On average, men are mugged more than women. Young men are twenty times more likely to be mugged than women or the elderly of either sex.

A Home Office report refers to parks, dances and parties as 'risk locations' and public transport and walking as 'dangerous travel'.

LIFE INSURANCE

Looking after yourself

The good news for dependents is that the average person is covered by a life insurance policy. The not-so-good news is that the average pay-out value is only £6,000.

8 EDUCATION ✓

PLAY SCHOOL

The average mother puts her children into (paid-for) play school before starting proper school at 5. Twenty per cent of mothers are working part-time.

The Japanese, probably taking their cue from the rising sun, start their infants off early in education, with the result that they are the most brained race: average IQ is 106.

PRIMARY SCHOOL

The average boy of between 9 and 12 likes to play football at playtime, tell jokes and discuss hairy-scary men and werewolves.

The average girl prefers to chat – about such topics as the miners, the royal family and kicking boys.

Boys are keen to go out as soon as it's breaktime, but 1 in 3 girls would be quite happy to stay in school all the time.

Boys drink more – probably because they run around more; girls eat more and spend more money if there's a sweet shop nearby.

SECONDARY SCHOOL

The average child, in 9 out of 10 cases, attends a state school, 1 in 17 attends an independent school and 1 in 72 attends a remedial or special school.

Nationally, 3 in 4 pupils attend a comprehensive school; double the number receiving this type of education 10 years ago.

Within the state system 1 in 5 attends a religious-based school, the Catholic schools – which are not confined to Catholic children – enjoying a particularly high reputation for good quality teaching and exam results.

MICRO-COMPUTERS

Give the little 'uns, little 'uns

Almost every school in England, Wales and Northern Ireland has a micro-computer. The average school has 9.

Almost 2 in 3 schools have a member of staff with responsibility for computing across the curriculum. The same percentage of schools have developed micro courses for 'computer awareness and appreciation'.

We have not yet located the mathematics class with 10 micros where the teacher was heard to say, 'If I take 3 micros away from 10 micros, how many am I left with?'

QUALIFICATIONS

In the UK the average academic qualification is a CSE certificate. 50 per cent of the working population possess this qualification. In Germany the equivalent qualification is gained by 66 per cent, in America by 75 per cent.

Mr Nigel Hawkins C . . . S . . . E . . .!

HOMEWORK

The average time children spend on homework is 18 minutes for boys and 38 minutes for girls. Nearly half the boys and a third of the girls say they do no homework at all.

VANDALS AND ABSENTEES

By crook or by hookey

An average of 30,000 children play truant every school day. This is apart from genuine absenteeism for medical and compassionate reasons.

A video recorder is stolen from a London school every day.

Vandalism, arson and theft cost schools £500 million a year. There is a serious indiscipline problem in nearly 500 secondary schools.

LEAVING SCHOOL

Most children leave school as soon as they're old enough. 3 pupils in 10 stay on – generally more girls than boys. Of those who leave:

1 in 6 leaves for full- or part-time education.
3 in 10 leave to get a job.
1 in 10 joins a government training scheme.
1 in 7 becomes unemployed.

Boys on average, even though they have no job to go to, seem to prefer the risk of unemployment to further education.

STAYING ON

Of those pupils who stay on at school, only 1 in 5 obtains one or more A levels. These poor results are attributed primarily to high pupil-teacher ratios – in the state school sector the average is 19 pupils per teacher. At independent schools there are 12.5 per teacher.

HIGHER EDUCATION

The average student does not go on to higher education at all. Only 1 in 3 does and twice as many from the south as from the north – with even fewer from the Midlands.

Independent schools, although educating only 6 per cent of all pupils, achieve 31 per cent of all university places – an average result more than 3 times better than the state schools.

Within the state system, comprehensives do twice as well as grammar schools in numbers sent to university.

AVERAGE STUDENT DEBTS

The average student has a bank account and an overdraft of about £100.

The National Union of Students reckon that up to 200,000 students may therefore currently face overdrafts totalling more than £13 million. Banks, however, are still pursuing students vigorously. One high street bank, for instance, aims to increase its slice of the student market by offering students a £6 cash gift plus free banking while studying. Student customers will have preferential overdrafts rates of 1 per cent over base rate on loans up to £100.

A MATTER OF DEGREE

The average number of students who obtain a first degree is 20 per cent in the UK. Germany has the same success rate; USA 33 per cent and Japan 40 per cent.

The UK bias is towards the Arts, the other countries towards Sciences. Perhaps in millenia to come we may be the only country who can draw or describe a car or camera – even though we couldn't make one.

Before you went to university you lacked the necessary qualifications.
Now I'm afraid you're overqualified.

RELIGION

RELIGIOUS BELIEFS

The average Briton is a Protestant. The UK is unique in having 6 major religions among its population. Per 1,000 people these are:

741	Proestants
194	Catholics
27	Muslims
18	Hindus
8	Jews
2	Orthodox Russian/Greek

Christianity is the major world religion. 25 per cent of the world's population is Christian in the proportion of 5 Catholics to 2 Protestants.

Now whether the concept of an Almighty Being confuses most of us, as it did the little boy who couldn't understand why god had the name of a swear word, the fact is: the avrage Briton does not go to church.

Religion?

Maybe it's because many of the so-called Protestants are those who simply put 'C of E' on enquiry forms because atheist or agnostic sounds so argumentative.

Here are average weekly attendances figures per 100:

- 7 Protestants
- 48 Catholics
- 6 Muslims
- 4 Hindus
- 4 Jews
- 1 Orthodox

The God-shaped blank within us seems to be growing. Membership of Britain's non-conformist churches has fallen below 1 million for the first time this century. They have lost more than 250,000 members in the last 10 years.

During the same period the Church of England has suffered a similar decline with regular church attendances dropping from 1.4 million to 1.2 million.

About 1.6 million Catholics attend Mass regularly – about 14 per cent down on the figure 10 years ago.

Overall this means an average of only one person in 15 regularly attends any place of worship.

But attendances are better in other religions. Over the last decade, the number of Muslims has doubled to almost 1 million, and the numbers of worshipping Sikhs and Hindus have also increased – by 50 per cent.

A QUESTION OF FAITH

Probably the low Christian attendances reflect our changing opinions. The average person is no longer certain of once fundamental Christian beliefs.

On the question of the Virgin Birth:

- 46 per cent think it is a legend
- 35 per cent think it is an historical fact
- 19 per cent are not sure

On the question of Jesus rising from the dead there is even more division:
- 34 per cent think He was raised bodily from the dead
- 33 per cent think the Resurrection was in a more spiritual way.

The remaining 34 per cent are either not sure, have no views or have another theory.

And yet 41 per cent of the UK population believe in UFOs – so we have a belief in something out there if not up there.

He insists it's more effective than Hail Marys.

POLITICS

I had no idea a week in politics would be such a long time.

AVERAGE VOTER

Although General de Gaulle said that politics are too serious a matter to be left to the politicians, it's not a sentiment that's crossed the Channel well. The average Briton is a sluggardly voter. We have one of the lowest turnouts at elections of any western country. Only the USA is lower.

Just 70 per cent of us are there at the polling booth at general election time; and half this figure vote at local and European elections.

AVERAGE VOTE

Using the last election as a base we can say that the average voter votes Tory. By which we mean only that more people voted for the Conservatives than for any other party.

But in truth, 60 per cent of the electorate voted against the current government (at the same time, the Austrian government, with 48 per cent of votes, resigned – because it did not consider that it commanded popular support).

To sort out our national political preferences is all much more difficult than it used to be – like Life and touching your toes. Until the late 70s Labour and Conservative could count on approximately 40 per cent each of the voting public. A 1 or 2 per cent swing was crucial.

The SDP has changed all that – at the moment at the expense of the Labour party, which gained only 28 votes for every 100 cast; the Alliance had 26 and the Conservatives 42 votes.

The UK is unique in the EEC in not having a coalition government.

The thing is, the Communists are dumb. Otherwise, why would they be Communists. So they probably wouldn't even *know* they were destroyed unless we did it about eight times.

AVERAGE PARTY MEMBERSHIP

Here the Tories really dominate, with paid-up membership between 1.8 and 2 million — which is 1 in 5 of the population over 18.

The average person is more than twice as likely to belong to the Conservative Party as any other party.

The second largest is the Alliance party with between 350,000 and 375,000 (split 300,000 Liberals and between 50–75,000 SDP) and a slowly rising membership.

Labour is third, with a falling membership — from about 450,000 in the 1950s to its present 300,000 members.

Communists are not doing at all well. Currently they have only about 20,000 members — a drop of 40 per cent in 20 years.

ALLIANCES

Political Sexcess

The Social Democratic Party may have sprung fully grown from the loins of the Labour party but certainly its sex life is more liberal. The average Alliance female supporter has a more active sex life than the average Conservative or Labour woman.

Not that here's a tale of unbridled libido — it's all well within average limits — even a bit on the low side. The average Alliance woman has sex twice a week compared with only 2 in 5 Labour supporters who do, and even fewer Tories.

It could be argued that the Lib-SDP woman had a better start — more Alliance supporters when girls were told the facts of life than either Tory or Labour youngsters. 6 in 10 Labour women, in fact, had to find out for themselves and perhaps some of them have not found out too much — only 1 in 4 Labour women has had more than one sexual partner compared with 1 in 3 Alliance women.

AVERAGE MP

An average MP is almost a contradiction in terms. As a group they are quite unrepresentative of the country's population: there are only 23 women and no Asians or blacks.

However, the definition of an honest politician as one who when he is bought, stays bought, seems unjust seeing that 1 MP in 3 is a lawyer or has a legal background.

1 in 2 Labour MPs are Union-sponsored and thus are known as TUMPs. 4 in 10 MPs have other jobs.

The House of Commons has seats for only 437 of its membership of 650. The average age of the full membership of the House of Lords is over 70.

157

A EURO MP IS . . . ?

The average person does not know much about
Euro MPs.

They have insinuated themselves on to the
far horizons of our political scene. We don't
know how many we have (it's 81), the total
number there are (there are 433), or quite how
many people they represent (the UK average
is 695,000 people).

And the awful truth appears to be . . . the
average person does not seem to care.

The man who said he'd voted in the Euro-elections.

?UIZ

Average questions

1. For every square kilometre of the respective country there are 231 Britons, 320 Japanese, 352 Dutch. How many Australians?

2. How many frowns before you make a wrinkle? 10 million? 2 million? 200,000? 10,000?

3. Which country has the airline with the best safety record? Australia? Scandinavia? Japan? America?

4. What is the average percentage of first class mail delivered the next day?

5. How many vehicles checked at random by the police are defective, on average? None? 10%? 20%? 30%?

6. The average Christmas tree is bugged. How many sundry midges, fleas, lice, spiders and beetles are concealed within its branches? 30? 300? 3,000? 30,000?

7. Nearly three-quarters of the UK land value is owned by – 42,000 people? 1.5 million people? 20 million people? 42 million people?

8. How many times a day do you blink, on average? 50? 1,000? 10,000? 25,000?

Average answers

1. 2 people per kilometre – no wonder they gave the world the phrase 'to go walkabout'.
2. 200,000 frowns before the evidence is there for good.
3. Australian Airlines with only 0.3 fatalities per million flights – Britain is fifth in the safety league.
4. 87%. How is it your mail is always in the late 13%?
5. 30%. 25% have trouble with their lights.
6. 30,000. But most of them die when the tree is taken inside.
7. 42,000 people – they are more than averagely rich.
8. 25,000. Blinking often isn't it?

Reference sources

United Nations Secretariat
Europe Yearbook (Europa
    Publications) Ltd.
International Labour Organization
World Health Organization
U.N.E.S.C.O.
INTERPOL
Social Trends 1984 (HMSO)
Family Expenditure Survey (Dept. of
    Employment)
Office of Population Censuses &
    Surveys
General Register Office (Scotland)
General Register Office (N. Ireland)
Home Office
General Household Survey (HMSO)
Dept. of Health & Social Security
Scottish Health Service
Welsh Office
Common Services Agency
Dept. of Education & Science
New Earnings Survey, Dept. of
    Employment
Central Statistical Office
Dept. of the Environment
Dept. of Transport
Ministry of Agriculture Fisheries &
    Food (National Food Survey)
Dept. of Trade & Industry
H.M. Customs & Excise
Manpower Services Commission
Scottish Education Dept.
Labour Force Survey
H.M. Govt. Actuary's Dept.
Inland Revenue (Survey of Personal
    Income)
Bank of England
Dept. of National Savings
Health & Safety Executive
Scottish Development Dept.
Dept. of Energy
H.M. Treasury
The Post Office
British Telecom
Trades Union Congress
BBC
IBA
British Rail
National Coal Board
Economic Intelligence Unit
Parole Board
English House Condition Survey
    (D.O.E.)
Joint Manpower Watch
British Tourist Authority
British Overseas Trade Board
The Market Research Society
Aylington Management
Arts Council
Eurostat

Euromonitor
'What People Earn' – P. Carpelli
    (MacDonald & Co.)
'Men at Work in Modern Britain' –
    David Weir, Ed. (Fontana)
'The Changing Anatomy of Britain' –
    Anthony Sampson (Coronet)
The Chartered Institute of Public
    Finance & Accountancy
The Newspaper Society
Verified Free Distribution Ltd.
JICNARS
Booksellers Association of G.B. &
    Ireland Ltd.
The Publishers Association
Survey 'Book Selling in a Cold
    Climate' (Booksellers/Publishers
    Assoc.)
Intercompany Comparison
Jordan's
The Bookseller
Publishing News
The Tablet
The Universe
The Jewish Chronicle
British Theatre Directory
Assoc. of British Travel Agents
Dover Docks & Harbour Board
Motor magazine
The Sports Council
The Countryside Commission
The Ramblers Association
English Golf Union
Rugby Football Union
Rugby League
Football League
Football Association
Scottish Football League
Scottish Football Association
Welsh Football Association
U.E.F.A.
F.I.F.A.
Test & County Cricket Board
Club Cricket Conference
Cyclists Touring Club
Autocycle Union
National Greyhound Racing Club Ltd.
The Jockey Club
Royal Yachting Assoc.
Society of Motor Manufacturers &
    Traders
AA
RAC
The British Insurance Association
British United Provident Association
Private Patients Plan
Western Provident Association
Survey 'Burial & Cremation Services'
    – H. J. Flynn (Frost & Sullivan)
Survey 'Industrial & Residential

Security Equipment' – H. J. Flynn
    (Frost & Sullivan)
Survey 'Motorcycle & Aftermarket in
    Europe' – H. J. Flynn (Frost &
    Sullivan)
Low Pay Unit
Survey 'Unequal Fringes' – Smail/
    Green/Hadjimatheon (L.P.U.)
Survey 'Low Pay in Scotland' – Fred.
    Twine (L.P.U.)
Survey 'Making Ends Meet' – Dominic
    Bryne (L.P.U.)
University Grants Committee
The Industrial Society
Interbank Research Organization
Midland Bank Ltd.
National Accounts of O.E.C.D.
    Countries
Forum magazine
Consumers' Association
Which? magazine
Woman magazine
Survey 'Love and the Unmarried
    Woman (*Woman* magazine)
Survey 'Love Life of the British Wife'
    (*Woman* magazine)
Survey 'Sex and the Under-Sixteens'
    (*Loving* magazine)
Survey 'Weddings' (*Brides & Setting
    Up Home* magazine)
Survey 'Wedding Bills' (*Wedding Day
    & First Home*' magazine)
Class – A. Marwick (Fontana)
Class – Jilly Cooper (Corgi)
British Medical Association
Health Education Council
Journal of the Royal College of General
    Practitioners
Community Health Dept. University of
    Leicester (Dr M E Preston-Whyte)
Readership Survey – (*Successful
    Slimming* magazine)
'Redundant Woman' – Angela Coyle
Housework Survey – (Gallup Poll)
J Walls & Sons Ltd.
Brewers Society
Alcoholics Anonymous
Samaritans
Tobacco Advisory Council
Charities Aid Foundation
The Times
Daily Mail
Financial Times
Daily Mirror
The Sunday Times
Daily Express
Newspaper Publishers Association
Audit Bureau of Circulation
National Readership Survey (A.B.C.)